Cooking with the Horse and Buggy People Series

Amish Community Cooking From Greenville, PA

FARMHOUSE

Kitchen

A GOOD FOOD HERITAGE

578

SELECT RECIPES

ISBN 978-1-933753-201

Photography: Nic Miller
Food Styling: Rosetta Wengerd
Book Design: Grace Troyer & Rosetta Mullet
Printed by: Carlisle Printing

Carlisle Press
WALNUT CREEK
800.852.4482
2673 Township Road 421
Sugarcreek, OH 44681

1–12014–5M
2–52014–10M

Introduction

My daughter Veronica and I enjoyed compiling
this cookbook of many tasty recipes from all the
exceptionally good cooks in our community. Currently we are
making church meals for 170 people and a favorite is always a
delicious salad made with romaine lettuce. 18 years ago Twila
Beachy and I compiled Walnut Creek Valley Cookbook, and
it is especially interesting for me now that I've moved out of
Holmes County, Ohio to use ladies' recipes that interacted with
me in my younger years.

Welcome to Farmhouse Kitchen! Browse through the many
delicious recipes and try something for dinner tonight. God
bless you as you reach out and share food with your friends and
neighbors!

-Naomi Mast

Dedication

My husband Matthias who has patiently eaten anything that we cook even when it flops. He is always grateful for a warm meal.

To my daughters Veronica, Rebekah and Rachel who are learning the art of cooking.

To my Mother, Esther who taught me to cook tasty meals.

To all the exceptionally good cooks who make many large meals for our community and have become dear friends of mine.

Table of Contents

V

Farmhouse Kitchen

Beverages and
Appetizers

Fruit Smoothies

MATTHIAS & NAOMI MAST

2 c. yogurt
1 c. strawberries
½ c. pineapple juice
¼ c. cane sugar
¼ c. blueberries
1 c. frozen peaches
1 frozen banana
1 Tbsp. lemon juice

Mix in blender until smooth.

Almond Milk

MATTHIAS & NAOMI MAST

3 c. water
½ c. almonds (blanched)

Blend in blender and strain twice. Sweetener and vanilla can be added.

2

Rice Milk

MATTHIAS & NAOMI MAST

7½ c. water, boiling
½ lb. rice flour
3 c. water
½ c. olive oil
1 Tbsp. sea salt
4 Tbsp. honey

Blend rice flour and 3 c. water. Stir into boiling water. Add olive oil, salt and honey. Simmer for 30 minutes. Add water to desired consistency. More sweetener may be added if desired.

Cappuccino

JAMES & IDA LEHMAN

8 c. coffee creamer
8 c. dry milk
4 c. instant hot chocolate mix
2 c. malted milk
1½ c. instant coffee
1 tsp. salt

Mix all ingredients together in 7 qt. mixing bowl. Store in a tight container. Use ¼ c. mix to 1 cup hot water. Serves 50 people.

Cappuccino Mix

MATTHIAS & NAOMI MAST

4 c. coffee creamer
2 c. dry milk
3 Tbsp. instant chocolate mix
2 c. sugar
½ tsp. cinnamon
½ tsp. salt
¾ c. Roma or instant coffee
1 c. malted milk

Measure all ingredients into blender and blend until fine. To serve: 2 heaping Tbsp. to a cup of hot water.

3

Iced Coffee

JAY & AMY TROYER, ROSALYN SCHLABACH

¾ c. sugar
½ c. instant coffee
1 Tbsp. vanilla flavoring
10 c. strongly brewed coffee
1 can sweetened condensed milk

Add sugar, instant coffee and vanilla to the brewed coffee. Stir, then add sweetened condensed milk. Cool. To serve, fill glass half full with ice and fill with coffee and milk mixture.

Beverages & Appetizers

Iced Coffee

RACHEL MAST, AGE 9

2 c. water
¾ c. cane sugar
½ c. french vanilla creamer
3 Tbsp. instant coffee

Heat water, sugar and instant coffee. Heat only to melt sugar. Fill gallon pitcher ½ full with ice. Put ½ of ice in a bowl and pour coffee mixture over ice to cool. Pour back into pitcher with remaining ice. Fill with milk and ½ cup french vanilla creamer. Can use Roma, a healthy coffee substitute.

Mocha Punch

LEAH KRISTINE TROYER, JUSTIN & NAOMI MILLER

4

1½ qt. water
½ c. instant chocolate
    drink mix
½ c. sugar
¼ c. instant coffee granules
½ gal. vanilla ice cream
½ gal. chocolate ice cream
8 oz. Cool Whip

In a large saucepan, bring water to boil. Remove from heat. Add drink mix, sugar and coffee. Stir until dissolved. Cover and refrigerate 4 hours or overnight. A half hour before serving, pour into punch bowl. Add ice cream by scoopfuls and stir until partially melted. Garnish with dollops of Cool Whip. Serves 12–15 people.

Lemonade

REBEKAH MAST, AGE 11

6½ c. water
1 c. ReaLemon
1 c. sugar

A simple and delicious drink on a warm day!

Fruit Punch

STEVE & MIRIAM LENGACHER

4 c. orange juice
2 c. pineapple juice
1 c. 7-Up
1 c. water

Mix and enjoy.

Orange Punch

ENOS & NANCY TROYER

3 (2 liters) 7-Up
3 (48 oz.) cans pineapple juice
3 (2 liters) ginger ale
3 qt. orange sherbet

Pour 7-Up, pineapple juice, and ginger ale into 24 qt. stock pot. Then add the sherbet and stir until it melts and is foamy. Very refreshing!

Homemade Root Beer

MATTHIAS & NAOMI MAST

2 c. sugar
2 Tbsp. root beer extract
1 tsp. yeast
1 gal. lukewarm water

Mix yeast and sugar with a little water. Let set for 5 minutes, then add root beer extract and the rest of the water. Set in the sun for 3–4 hours. Do not turn lid tight. Store in a cold place.

5

Hot Chocolate Mix

LARRY & NAOMI LENGACHER

30 oz. Nestle Quik
2 lb. powdered sugar
18–20 oz. coffee creamer
25.6 oz. powdered milk

Mix everything together. If not sweet enough, add more powdered sugar, or if not enough flavor, add more chocolate. Use ⅓ cup to 1 cup hot water.

Chocolate Milk

CALEB DUANE WEAVER

1 c. milk
½ c. sugar
¼ c. cocoa
1 gal. milk

Heat 1 c. milk. Add sugar and cocoa. Stir until dissolved. Pour into a gallon of milk and mix.

Chocolate Syrup

JOSEPH & RHODA MILLER

1 c. water
1 c. brown sugar
1 c. white sugar
¼ tsp. salt
4 Tbsp. cocoa
1 tsp. vanilla

Heat first 5 ingredients to boiling; take off heat and add vanilla. We like to use this for chocolate milk.

6

Tortilla Pinwheels

JAY & AMY TROYER

16 oz. sour cream
8 oz. cream cheese
1 pkg. ranch mix
onions
bacon
shredded cheese
8 tortillas

Mix ingredients and spread on tortillas. Roll up tightly and refrigerate several hours before cutting. Slice about ¾" thick.

Cheese Ball

JUSTIN & NAOMI MILLER

2 (8 oz.) pkg. cream cheese
1 c. cheddar cheese
1 Tbsp. parsley flakes
1 Tbsp. onions
1 tsp. ReaLemon
2 tsp. Worcestershire sauce
dried beef (optional)

Mix all ingredients. Roll in a ball. Cover with parsley flakes and chopped nuts. Spread on crackers and enjoy.

Cheese Ball

MARCUS & ROSANNA MAST

2 (8 oz.) pkg. cream cheese
2 c. cheddar cheese
2 tsp. Worcestershire sauce
½ tsp. garlic salt
½ tsp. onion salt
Lawry's seasoning salt
¼ c. parsley flakes
¼ c. chopped nuts

Mix everything together except nuts and parsley flakes. Form into a ball and roll in nuts and parsley flakes.

7

Cheese Ball

MATTHIAS & NAOMI MAST

2 (8 oz.) pkg. cream cheese
8½ oz. crushed pineapples,
    drained
2 Tbsp. diced onions
parsley flakes

Chill ½ hour before shaping.

Cheese Ball

MATTHIAS & NAOMI MAST

2 (8 oz.) pkg. cream cheese,
    softened
10 slices bacon, fried & chopped
⅓ c. onion
½ c. red &/or green pepper
8 oz. cheddar cheese
½ c. Miracle Whip
1 Tbsp. lemon juice
¼ tsp. garlic salt

Mix together all ingredients and shape into ball. Serve with crackers.

8

Chocolate Chip Cheese Ball

JACOB & LORETTA WEAVER

½ c. butter, softened
    (no substitute)
8 oz. cream cheese, softened
¼ tsp. vanilla
¾ c. powdered sugar
2 Tbsp. brown sugar
¾ c. mini chocolate chips
¾ c. chopped pecans
graham crackers

Mix all together except pecans and crackers. Refrigerate 2 hours. Place on plastic wrap and shape into ball. Roll into pecans and refrigerate another hour. Serve with graham crackers.

Cream Cheese Salsa Dip

VERNON & RUTH YODER

8 oz. cream cheese
16 oz. sour cream
1 pkg. taco seasoning
1 (12 oz.) jar salsa
8 oz. shredded cheese

Mix cream cheese, sour cream and taco seasoning. Spread in a flat container. Put salsa on top. Put shredded cheese on top. Serve with chips.

Mexican Hamburger Dip

MARY LENGACHER

2 lb. hamburger, browned
1 med. onion, chopped
½ green pepper, chopped
1 (15 oz.) can refried beans
1 can cream of mushroom soup
1 can tomato soup
1 lb. Velveeta cheese

Add any or all of these seasonings: taco seasoning, chili powder, garlic salt or powder and red pepper. I usually use 1 Tbsp. taco seasoning, 1 tsp. chili powder and 1 tsp. garlic powder. Mix together well and simmer for 25-30 minutes. Serve with tortilla chips.

Bean Dip - from Mexico

MARY LENGACHER

1 can black-eyed peas
1 can shoe peg corn
1 can pinto beans
1 green pepper
½ c. red onion
½ jar pimentos

Sauce:
1 c. sugar
½ c. vinegar
¼ c. olive oil

Drain and rinse peas, corn and beans. Finely chop pepper and onion. Mix together, then add the pimentos. *Sauce:* Boil together ingredients. Cool. Then pour over bean mixture. Serve with scoop-like chips. Keeps a long time in refrigerator.

Note: Optional: can add a little jalapeño juice.

9

Hamburger Chip Dip

STEVE & MIRIAM LENGACHER

2 lb. hamburger
1 can tomato soup
1 can cream of mushroom soup
1 sm. onion, chopped
1 green pepper, chopped
2 lb. Velveeta cheese, or less
1 pkg. taco seasoning
salt & pepper to taste

Fry hamburger, onion and pepper. Add your soups and cheese. Stir in taco seasoning, salt and pepper as desired. Makes a large amount.

Note: You can also put in crockpot to keep warm.

Honey Teriyaki Dip

JOHN & ESTA YODER

8 oz. cream cheese, softened
1 c. cooked & diced chicken
4 green onions, chopped
1 Tbsp. powdered garlic
½ c. chopped peanuts (optional)
¼ c. honey teriyaki sauce

Mix garlic and cream cheese together. Spread on plate. Top with chicken, onions and peanuts; drizzle with sauce. Chill. Serve with sesame crackers. Serves 6 to 8.

10

Taco Dip

STEVIE & REBECCA SWAREY

2 (8 oz.) pkg. cream cheese,
    softened
12 oz. cottage cheese
1 pkg. taco seasoning
browned hamburger
onion, lettuce, tomatoes,
    olives, cheese

Whip in blender; add 1-2 Tbsp. milk if too stiff. Spread on plate; top with toppings. Serve with tortilla chips. Delicious!

Taco Chip Dip

JAY & AMY TROYER

16 oz. sour cream
8 oz. cream cheese
½ pkg. taco seasoning
½ bottle taco sauce
¾ c. salsa
cheddar cheese, shredded
green peppers, finely cut
lettuce (optional)
bacon

Mix together sour cream, cream cheese and taco seasoning for first layer; pour taco sauce and salsa over first layer, then top with cheddar cheese, peppers and bacon. Shredded lettuce may also be used on top.

Hot Taco Dip

MATTHIAS & NAOMI MAST

8 oz. cream cheese, softened
16 oz. sour cream
8 oz. taco sauce
taco seasoning
1 sm. onion (optional)
1 green pepper
8 oz. shredded cheddar
lettuce & tomatoes

Beat cream cheese until smooth, add sour cream, taco sauce and taco seasoning. Put mixture on platter and top with lettuce, tomatoes, peppers, onions and cheddar cheese. Serve with nacho chips.

11

Herb Garlic Spread

JUSTIN & NAOMI MILLER

2 (8 oz.) pkg. cream cheese,
  softened
¼ c. butter, softened
½ tsp. basil
½ tsp. oregano
½ tsp. thyme
½ tsp. marjoram
½ tsp. dill weed
½ tsp. garlic powder
½ tsp. pepper
1 c. shredded cheddar cheese

Mix well. Spread on crackers and enjoy!

Caramel Apple Dip

JENNIFER MILLER

¾ c. brown sugar
8 oz. cream cheese
1 tsp. vanilla
¾ c. sour cream

Mix all together. Serve with apples or any other fresh fruit.

Apple Dip

JAY & AMY TROYER

8 oz. cream cheese
¾ c. brown sugar
1 tsp. vanilla
marshmallow creme or
  Cool Whip

Beat cream cheese; add other ingredients and beat.

12

Fruit Dip

MATTHIAS & NAOMI MAST

2 (8 oz.) pkg. cream cheese,
  softened
16 oz. Cool Whip
3 c. strawberry yogurt
¼ c. strawberry jam
¾ c. cane sugar
  (powdered in blender)

Mix cream cheese with sugar; gradually add Cool Whip, yogurt and jam.

Fruit Dip

IVAN & BARBARA SCHLABACH

18 oz. strawberry yogurt
8 oz. cream cheese, softened
8 oz. Cool Whip
1 c. sugar

Mix all together. Freezes well. Yield: 6 c.

Fruit Dip

13

ED & MARY SLABAUGH

8 oz. cream cheese, softened
1 c. marshmallow creme
8 oz. whipped topping
¼ c. dry Jell-O

Mix well.

Fruit Dip

MONICA LENGACHER

12 oz. Cool Whip
1½ c. powdered sugar
8 oz. cream cheese
pineapple juice

Combine and add enough pineapple juice for dipping consistency. Good with fresh pineapple, apples, grapes, etc.

Creamy Caramel Dip

JOSIAH & SUSAN MILLER

8 oz. cream cheese, softened
¾ c. brown sugar, packed
1 c. sour cream
2 tsp. vanilla
2 tsp. lemon juice
1 c. cold milk
3 oz. instant vanilla pudding

In a mixing bowl, beat cream cheese and brown sugar until smooth. Add the sour cream, vanilla, lemon juice, milk and pudding mix, beating well after each addition. Cover and chill for at least 1 hour. Serve as dip for fruit. Yield: 3½ c.

Mustard Dip

MATTHEW & MARLENE TROYER

1 c. sour cream
1 c. mayonnaise
½ c. mustard
½ c. sugar
2 Tbsp. dried onion
½ tsp. horseradish sauce
1 pkg. ranch mix (dry)

Mix and serve with pretzels and crackers. Serves 6.

14

Our Family's Favorite Cracker Spread

REGINA ROSE TROYER

2 (8 oz.) pkg. cream cheese
2 tsp. minced garlic
3 tsp. minced onion
6 Tbsp. butter
½ c. brown sugar
3 tsp. brown & spicy mustard
1 Tbsp. Worcestershire sauce
1½ c. pecans

Mix first 3 ingredients and shape on a plate. Heat the rest of the ingredients till melted. Cool, then put on cream cheese mixture. Serve with crackers. Serves 8.

Tuna Dip

ED & MARY SLABAUGH

1 (6 oz.) can tuna, drained &
   flaked
8 oz. cream cheese, softened
3 tsp. lemon juice
4 drops hot pepper sauce

Can be made into a ball and rolled in parsley. For a dip, add salad dressing until it has the right consistency.

Chocolate Lovers' Dip

JOHN & ESTA YODER

8 oz. whipped topping
1 c. chocolate chips
Rumex extract

Melt chocolate chips; cool. Mix with whipped topping; add a few drops Rumex extract. Serve with strawberries, pineapple, apples or any fruit you prefer.

15

RECIPE FOR _____

_____

_____

_____

_____

_____

_____

_____

_____

_____

_____

_____

RECIPE FOR _____

_____

_____

_____

_____

_____

_____

_____

_____

_____

_____

_____

_____

Breads and Rolls

Honey Wheat Bread

JAMES & IDA LEHMAN

4½ c. hot water
¾ c. honey
1 c. vegetable oil
1½ Tbsp. salt
5 c. wheat flour
5 Tbsp. wheat gluten
3 Tbsp. lecithin
¼ c. yeast, heaping
6 c. wheat flour

Using 6 qt. mixer, mix first 8 ingredients and let set for ½ hour. Gradually add 6 c. flour with mixer set on '2'; knead for 10 minutes. Remove dough from mixer on lightly greased countertop. Divide dough into 5 parts and form loaves. Place in greased pans and let rise for approx. 45 minutes. Bake at 350° until golden brown.

Wheat Bread

JOSIAH & RHODA MILLER

1 c. warm water
2 Tbsp. yeast
1 Tbsp. sugar
2 Tbsp. lecithin
2 Tbsp. wheat gluten
⅔ c. olive oil
⅔ c. honey
3 tsp. salt
3 c. hot water
9 c. wheat flour
2-3 c. white flour

Mix 1 c. warm water with yeast and sugar. Let set. In large bowl, mix rest of ingredients except the flour. Stir well; add 4 c. wheat flour. Mix well. Then gradually add rest of flour. Let rise for 30 minutes, then punch down and let rise for another 30 minutes. Roll out and put in pans and let rise again. Bake at 350° for approx. 25-30 minutes. Yield: 4 large loaves or 5 smaller loaves.

Bread

JOSEPH & RHODA MILLER

3 c. warm water
2 Tbsp. yeast
1 Tbsp. salt
¾ c. brown sugar
¾ c. whole wheat flour
¾ c. vegetable oil
2 Tbsp. lecithin
2 Tbsp. honey
1 egg
2 c. whole wheat flour
1 c. Occident flour

Mix first 5 ingredients and let set for 15 minutes. Add vegetable oil, lecithin, honey, beaten egg and Occident flour. Mix well before adding remaining flour. Let rise 30 minutes. Knead, let rise 1 hour. Put in pans. Let rise and bake at 300° for approx. 30 minutes. Yield: 4 loaves.

Batter Bread

JAMES & IDA LEHMAN

1 Tbsp. yeast
½ c. warm water
1 c. warm milk (115°)
½ c. vegetable oil
¼ c. honey
2 tsp. salt
2 eggs
5½-6 c. flour

In 7 qt. bowl, combine yeast and warm water. Add milk, vegetable oil, honey and salt; stir well. Add eggs and 3 c. flour; beat until smooth. Stir in remaining flour to form a soft dough. (Do not knead.) Cover, let rise till double. Stir the dough down. Spoon into 2 greased bread pans. Cover, let rise 1 hour. Bake at 375° for 30 minutes or until golden brown. Good to start in the afternoon and ready to serve fresh warm bread for supper.

19

Zucchini Bread

JOSIAH & RHODA MILLER, LUKE & KATHRYN MILLER

3 eggs
1½ c. sugar
1 Tbsp. vanilla
1 c. vegetable oil
1 Tbsp. cinnamon
2 tsp. soda
1 tsp. salt
¼ tsp. baking powder
2 c. sifted flour
   (sift flour then measure)
2 c. grated, unpeeled zucchini
1 c. chopped nuts

Beat together eggs, sugar, vanilla and vegetable oil. Add dry ingredients and mix well. Last add zucchini and nuts. Pour into 2 small bread pans. Bake at 325° for 1 hour or maybe a bit longer. Let set for 5-10 minutes, then remove from pans, and put glaze on top.

Glaze:
2 Tbsp. butter, softened
⅓ c. powdered sugar
½ tsp. almond flavoring
couple drops of water

Banana Bread

20

MICHAEL & JOANNE COBLENTZ

1¼ c. sugar
1 tsp. salt
1¼ tsp. soda
2½ c. flour
1 tsp. cinnamon
1 c. instant vanilla pudding
5 eggs
1 c. vegetable oil
1 tsp. vanilla
2 c. mashed bananas

Mix all dry ingredients together. In separate bowl beat together eggs, vegetable oil, vanilla and bananas. Add to dry ingredients and mix together just until moistened. Pour into 2 greased loaf pans. Bake at 325° for 65 minutes or more. Cool 10 minutes, then put on racks.

Banana Nut Bread

JOHN & ESTA YODER

1 c. shortening
2 c. sugar
4 eggs
6 mashed bananas
4 c. flour
1 tsp. soda
1 tsp. baking powder
1 c. chopped walnuts
1 tsp. salt

Cream shortening and sugar; add beaten eggs. Add dry ingredients alternately with bananas. Stir in nuts. Put into 2 greased loaf pans. Bake at 350° for approx. 1 hour.

Butterhorns

ATLEE & MATTIE MILLER

2 cans crescent rolls
8 oz. cream cheese, softened
4 Tbsp. honey

Mix cream cheese and honey together. Unfold crescents and put 1 Tbsp. mixture on each piece and roll up. Sprinkle with cinnamon if desired. Bake at 375° for 12-14 minutes, till golden brown. Serves 12. Delicious.

Melt-in-Your-Mouth Dinner Rolls

JAMES & IDA LEHMAN

2 pkg. dry yeast
1 c. warm water
2 Tbsp. sugar
2 tsp. baking powder
⅔ c. vegetable oil
2 c. milk, scalded
⅔ c. honey
dash of salt
4 eggs, beaten
9 c. flour

Dissolve yeast in warm water. Add next 2 ingredients and let set for 20 minutes. Scald milk, mix with vegetable oil, honey and salt and cool. Add eggs and yeast mixture to milk; add flour, stir with spoon, as it is very sticky. Cover and refrigerate 6 hours or overnight. Shape into balls and place in 2 (9"x13") pans. Let rise 2 hours. Bake at 350° until golden. Serves 30.

22

Dinner Rolls

STEVIE & REBECCA SWAREY

1 c. lard
1 c. sugar
2 eggs
4 tsp. salt
4 c. warm water
3 Tbsp. yeast
9-11 c. flour

Mix together first 4 ingredients till creamy. Add rest of ingredients. Yield: 4 doz.

Mushroom Loaf

MATTHEW & MARLENE TROYER

1 round loaf of French bread
¼ c. butter, melted
1 Tbsp. minced onion
1½ tsp. poppy seeds
2 minced garlic cloves
½ tsp. seasoned salt
½ tsp. ground mustard
½ tsp. lemon juice
mushrooms
Swiss cheese

Cut bread in squares (small) from top to bottom crust. Do not cut through crust. Fill cuts with sliced mushrooms and Swiss cheese. Melt together the rest of ingredients and pour over loaf. Wrap in foil and bake at 350° for 40 minutes. Serves 10.

Garlic Biscuits like Red Lobster

MATTHIAS & NAOMI MAST

2 c. Bisquick mix
½ c. shredded cheddar cheese
⅛ tsp. parsley flakes
⅔ c. milk
½ c. butter
½ tsp. garlic powder

Bake at 450° for 8-10 minutes. Melt butter and garlic powder and spread on finished biscuits. Bake immediately or they lose their texture.

23

Cheddar Cheese Muffins

JAMES & IDA LEHMAN

2½ c. flour
2 tsp. baking powder
½ tsp. baking soda
½ tsp. salt
1 tsp. dried basil
½ tsp. oregano
2 Tbsp. sugar
2½ c. grated cheddar cheese,
    divided
1 Tbsp. chopped onion
1½ c. buttermilk or sour milk
1 egg
½ c. vegetable oil

Mix first 7 ingredients. Add 2 c. cheese and onions; mix well. Whisk together milk, eggs and vegetable oil. Pour into dry ingredients, stir till just mixed. Spoon into 2 well-greased muffin tins. Sprinkle tops of muffins with remaining cheese. Bake at 370° for 20 minutes. Serve warm with your choice of soup. Serves 18.

Popular Muffins — Betty Crocker

MARY LENGACHER

2 c. flour
¼ c. sugar
3 tsp. baking powder
1 tsp. salt
1 egg
1 c. milk
¼ c. vegetable oil

Mix together dry ingredients. Beat egg with fork. Add milk and vegetable oil and add to dry mixture. Stir lightly, just till mixed. Batter should be lumpy. Fill muffin cups ⅔ full. Bake at 400° for 20 minutes or until golden brown. Serve warm. Yield: 12 muffins.

Betty Crocker Biscuits

MARY LENGACHER

2 c. flour
3 tsp. baking powder
1 tsp. salt
¼ c. shortening
¾ c. milk

Mix dry ingredients in bowl. Cut in shortening. Add milk (too much milk makes dough sticky-not enough makes biscuits dry). Knead lightly on floured surface. Handle lightly. Roll dough about ½" thick, cut with biscuit cutter. Place on ungreased baking sheet. Bake at 425° for 10-12 minutes.

Biscuits

SAMUEL & LEANNA WEAVER

2 c. flour
3 tsp. baking powder
1 tsp. salt
½ c. vegetable oil
¾ c. buttermilk

Blend dry ingredients. Pour liquid in together and mix. Drop on greased cookie sheet. Bake at 350°. Serves 8.

25

Creamy Chive Ring

JOSIAH & SUSAN MILLER

1 Tbsp. instant yeast
¼ c. warm water
1 c. milk
6 Tbsp. butter
¼ c. instant potato flakes or
    mashed potatoes
⅓ c. sugar
1 egg, well beaten
1¼ tsp. salt
3¾-4¼ c. flour

Filling:
1 egg, beaten
¾ c. rich cream
⅓ c. chives
½ tsp. salt

Dissolve yeast in warm water. Heat milk, butter, potatoes, sugar, egg and salt, not to boiling; cool to room temperature and add yeast and flour. Let rise till double and divide into 2 and roll into 16x12 rectangle. Divide filling and spread on dough; roll up and seal edges and put into greased pan, forming into wreath; cut in slits. Bake at 350° for 20-25 minutes. *Filling:* Heat on double boiler till thick, cool a bit. Spread on dough.

Cheesy Cornbread Muffins

JACOB & LORETTA WEAVER

1 c. flour
1 c. cornmeal
½ tsp. salt
3 tsp. baking powder
1 c. milk
1 egg
¼ c. vegetable oil
diced cheese bits
garlic powder
chili powder
onions, diced, or onion powder
green pepper, diced (optional)

Mix together dry ingredients; add vegetable oil, milk and egg. Add desired amount of cheese, onions, peppers and seasonings. Grease muffin pan; fill cups ½ full and bake at 400° until golden. Serve warm. Very good with chili soup.

26

Golden Cornbread

SAMUEL & LEANNA WEAVER, JACOB & LORETTA WEAVER

1 c. flour
1 c. cornmeal
4 tsp. baking powder
½ tsp. salt
1 egg
1 c. milk
¼ c. vegetable oil
¼ c. sugar

Mix dry ingredients; add egg, milk and vegetable oil. Pour into 9" square pan. Bake at 425° for 20-25 minutes. Recipe times 2 fills 9"x13" pan better. We like this with milk, a little sweetener and blueberries, peaches or strawberries (fresh or frozen). Also with chili soup. For muffins, you may add cheese, chopped onions and peppers. Omit sugar. Also, while it's hot, slice the tops off and butter and eat! Serves 8.

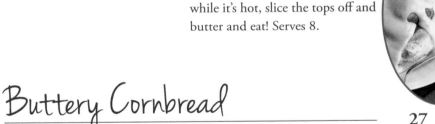

Buttery Cornbread

JOSEPH & RHODA MILLER

⅔ c. butter
1 c. sugar
3 eggs
1⅔ c. milk
1⅓ c. flour
1 c. cornmeal
4½ tsp. baking powder
1 tsp. salt

Preheat oven to 400°. In a mixing bowl, cream butter and sugar. Combine eggs and milk. Separately combine flour, cornmeal, baking powder and salt. Add egg and cornmeal mixtures alternately to butter and sugar mixture. Pour into a greased 9"x13" pan. Bake for 22-27 minutes. Serves 10.

Note: This is a favorite of ours served with Pizza Soup, also submitted in this cookbook.

Mexican Cornbread

JOSIAH & RHODA MILLER

2 pkg. cornbread muffin mix
  (8½ oz. each)
1 med. onion, chopped
2 c. shredded cheddar cheese
1 (14¾ oz.) can cream style corn
1½ c. sour cream
4 eggs, beaten
1 (4 oz.) can chopped green chilies
⅓ c. vegetable oil

In a bowl, combine cornbread mix and onion. Combine the remaining ingredients; add to the cornbread mixture, mixing just until moistened. Pour into a greased 9"x13" pan. Bake at 350° for 50-55 minutes or until lightly browned and the edges pull away from sides of pan. Serves 18 to 24.

Cornbread

ED & MARY SLABAUGH

1½ c. flour
1½ c. cornmeal
¾ c. sugar
1 tsp. salt
4 tsp. baking powder
½ c. olive oil
2 eggs
milk to make like cake batter

Mix all together in order given. Pour in a 9"x13" pan. Bake at 425°.

28

Spaghetti Bread

MICHAEL & JOANNE COBLENTZ

1 c. warm water
2 Tbsp. vegetable oil
⅓ c. Parmesan cheese
1 Tbsp. sugar
1 tsp. garlic powder
1 tsp. salt
¼ tsp. oregano
⅛ tsp. basil
⅛ tsp. marjoram
⅛ tsp. savory
⅛ tsp. thyme
⅛ tsp. rubbed sage
⅛ tsp. rosemary
1 Tbsp. yeast
2½ c. bread flour

Mix all together and add enough flour to make a nice dough. Let rise until double. Form a long loaf and put on large cookie sheet. Let rise again till double. Bake at 375° for 25-30 minutes. *Ranch Butter:* Mix butter with seasonings. Slice bread and butter each piece and put back together. Wrap whole loaf in tinfoil and warm slightly before serving.

Ranch Butter:
1 c. butter, softened
1 tsp. salt
1 tsp. parsley flakes
¼ tsp. garlic powder
¼ tsp. onion powder
½ tsp. black pepper

29

Herbed Oatmeal Pan Bread

JOSIAH & SUSAN MILLER

1½ c. boiling water
1 c. quick oats
3 Tbsp. butter
¼ c. sugar
2 tsp. salt
½ c. water
2 Tbsp. yeast
1 egg, lightly beaten
4 c. flour

Mix together quick oats, butter, sugar, salt and boiling water till butter is melted, then add egg, water, yeast and flour. Melt ¼ c. butter and spread on top of dough and sprinkle seasonings on top. Put on large cookie sheet. Bake at 375° for 15 minutes.

Seasonings:
2 Tbsp. Parmesan cheese   ½ tsp. oregano
1 Tbsp. basil   ½ tsp. garlic salt

30

Breadsticks

JOSIAH & RHODA MILLER

1 Tbsp. vegetable oil
2 c. water
1½ tsp. salt
2 Tbsp. sugar
1 Tbsp. yeast
4 c. flour

Mix yeast, water and sugar. Let set 5 minutes. Add salt and vegetable oil; stir. Add flour and let rise in bowl for around 20 minutes. Roll out onto a large cookie sheet (12"x17" pan). Spread dough with the topping mixture, cut in strips and let rise 20 minutes. Bake at 350° for approx. 20 minutes.

Topping:
½ c. melted butter
1 tsp. garlic powder
2 tsp. parsley flakes
2 tsp. Italian seasoning
3 Tbsp. Parmesan cheese

Breadsticks

JACOB & LORETTA WEAVER

1½ c. warm water
1 Tbsp. yeast
1 Tbsp. sugar
1¼ tsp. salt
3 Tbsp. vegetable oil
3¾ c. flour

Butter Mixture:
¾ c. butter, melted
3 Tbsp. Parmesan cheese
1 Tbsp. garlic powder
1 Tbsp. parsley flakes
1 Tbsp. Italian seasoning

Mix dough ingredients well. Grease 11"x17" pan and press dough evenly into pan. Cut into strips of desired size. Spread butter and seasonings over top, coating all the dough. Let rise a little. Bake at 325° for 15-20 minutes or until golden. Do not overbake!

31

Italian Breadsticks

JAY & AMY TROYER

2 Tbsp. yeast
1½ c. warm water
¼ c. sugar
4½ c. flour
1½ tsp. garlic salt
1 tsp. basil
1½ tsp. oregano

Butter Mixture:
½ c. butter
½ c. Italian dressing

Seasoning Mixture:
1 pkg. Italian dressing mix
salt
garlic salt
oregano
Italian seasoning
onion salt

Mix together first 7 ingredients. Press dough in pans. Cut in strips and top with butter mixture, then with seasoning mixture. Bake at 375°. After baked, sprinkle with cheddar or mozzarella cheese. Put in oven until cheese is melted. Enjoy!

32

Breadsticks

JAY & AMY TROYER

1½ c. warm water
1 Tbsp. yeast
1 Tbsp. sugar
1¼ tsp. salt
¼ c. vegetable oil
4 c. flour

Butter Mixture:
¾ c. butter
1 tsp. garlic powder
1 Tbsp. parsley
1 Tbsp. Italian seasoning

Parmesan cheese

Combine water and yeast and allow to dissolve. Add remaining ingredients. Let rise until double. Press into air-bake pan. Cut into 1"x4½" strips. Melt butter, spread on dough, sprinkle with seasonings and Parmesan cheese. Let rise and bake at 350° for 12-14 minutes. Serve warm. You can bake them ahead and freeze. Thaw and dip into melted butter again and bake until warm. Yield: Approx. 50 breadsticks.

Italian Breadsticks

MATTHIAS & NAOMI MAST

1 Tbsp. instant yeast
⅓ c. warm water
1 tsp. sugar
1 c. cold water
1½ Tbsp. vegetable oil
1 Tbsp. sugar
¼ tsp. garlic salt
1 tsp. oregano
½ tsp. salt
3½ c. flour

Mix together first 3 ingredients and let set for 5 minutes. Add rest of ingredients. Knead until smooth and elastic. Roll out and spread with Italian dressing and 2 c. mozzarella cheese. Bake in an 11"x17" pan at 450° till golden.

Soft Pretzels

MATTHIAS & NAOMI MAST

2 c. warm water
2 Tbsp. yeast
4 Tbsp. brown sugar
¼ c. vegetable oil
6 c. flour

Drop into 2 Tbsp. soda and boiling water before baking.

French Garlic Bread

JOSEPH & RHODA MILLER, IVAN & BARBARA SCHLABACH

2 c. warm water
2 Tbsp. yeast
2 Tbsp. sugar
⅔ c. Parmesan cheese
2 Tbsp. garlic powder
2 tsp. salt
½ tsp. oregano
⅛ tsp. basil
⅛ tsp. thyme
4 Tbsp. vegetable oil
5 c. flour

½ c. butter
½ tsp. garlic salt
1 tsp. Nature's salt

Mix water, yeast, sugar and salt. Let set for 15 minutes, then add cheese, seasonings, vegetable oil and 2 c. flour. Beat well before adding remaining flour. Let rise. Knead every 10 minutes, forming loaves the fifth time. Bake at 350° for 25-30 minutes. Cool, slice and spread butter mixture on each side. Wrap sliced loaf in foil and warm before serving. Yield: 2 loaves.

34

Pecan Rolls

ED & MARY SLABAUGH

2 c. warm water
½ c. milk
1 c. sugar
½ c. butter or margarine
3 eggs
3 tsp. salt
1½ Tbsp. yeast
½ c. warm

Syrup:
2 c. brown sugar
⅓ c. corn syrup
¼ c. butter or margarine
¼ c. water

1 c. pecans (optional)

Dissolve yeast in ½ c. warm water, then add to the rest of liquids, sugar, butter and eggs, and enough flour for easy mixing; beat till bubbly, then add flour to make a soft workable dough. Let rise until double. When ready to put rolls in pans, using 6 (9") pans, put ⅓ c. of syrup (bring syrup ingredients just to boiling point) in bottom and top with chopped pecans. Place rolls on top of this. Bake at 350° for 20 minutes or until lightly browned. When done, place upside down on a plate. Needs no icing. Yield: 6 pans.

35

Cinnamon Rolls

JUSTIN & NAOMI MILLER

1 c. warm water
2 Tbsp. yeast
1 c. sugar
2 tsp. salt
⅓ c. margarine or butter
⅓ c. vegetable oil
1½ c. milk, scalded
2 eggs
7¼ c. flour

Frosting:
1 c. butter
1 c. sugar
1 c. brown sugar
½ c. milk

Combine warm water and yeast in a small bowl. Mix all ingredients together. Dough should be fairly sticky. Let rise until double. Roll out and spread with butter, cinnamon and brown sugar. Roll up and cut. Let rise for 45 minutes. Bake at 350° for 20 minutes. Cook together frosting ingredients. Let cool a bit, then add powdered sugar. Yield: 28-30 rolls.

36

Cinnamon Rolls

MATTHIAS & NAOMI MAST

1 c. quick oats
2 c. boiling water
3 Tbsp. butter
⅔ c. brown sugar
1½ tsp. salt
2 Tbsp. dry yeast
⅓ c. warm water
1 Tbsp. cane sugar
5 c. bread flour

Cook together oatmeal, water and butter; let cool and pour over brown sugar and salt. When this is lukewarm add mixture of yeast, warm water and cane sugar. Dissolve and mix all together. Add flour, 1 c. at a time. Let rise once. Roll out and spread with butter, cinnamon and brown sugar or pie filling; roll up and cut. Place rolls into greased pans and bake at 350° till golden brown. Frost with favorite frosting.

Simple Cinnamon Rolls

MATTHIAS & NAOMI MAST

9-10 c. donut mix
3 c. warm water
2 Tbsp. yeast

Crumbs:
2 c. brown sugar
6 tsp. cinnamon

Sour Cream Icing:
½ c. butter
1 c. sour cream
1 c. brown sugar

Put water and yeast in Bosch or other mixer; mix together, gradually adding donut mix till smooth and elastic. Let rise to double; roll out; spread with melted butter. Sprinkle with brown sugar and cinnamon. Roll up and slice 1" thick. Put in pans and let rise. Bake at 350° for 15-20 minutes. *For Sour Cream Icing:* Melt together. Cool.

Apple Cinnamon Coffee Cake

MATTHIAS & NAOMI MAST

See preceding recipe for dough ingredients and instructions. Roll out dough. Spread with melted butter. Sprinkle with cinnamon and brown sugar, then cover with a thin layer of apple pie filling. Flip ½ of dough over on top of the other ½. Using a pizza cutter or chopper, chop into lots of small pieces. Place about 1½" layer in bottom of round pan. Sprinkle with brown sugar and cinnamon. Let rise. Bake at 350° for 30 minutes or till golden brown. Glaze with 1 c. powdered sugar and 2 Tbsp. water or milk or ice with sour cream icing.

37

Pumpkin Cinnamon Rolls

LARRY & NAOMI LENGACHER

1½ c. milk, scalded
1 c. pumpkin
½ c. sugar
2 tsp. salt
½ c. shortening
2 eggs, beaten
2 Tbsp. yeast
½ c. warm water
7 c. flour (more if needed)

Put sugar, salt and shortening in bowl; mix. Pour milk over top; add eggs, water and pumpkin, then yeast and flour. Do not make too stiff. Frost with your favorite frosting.

Cinnamon Rolls

STEVE & MIRIAM LENGACHER

2 c. scalded milk
2 c. lukewarm water
3 Tbsp. dry yeast
4 eggs, beaten
1 c. margarine or butter
1 c. sugar
3 tsp. salt
8½ c. flour

Dissolve yeast in water. Pour scalded milk over all other ingredients, except flour. Add yeast and mix. Work in flour. Cover and let rise till double. Roll out and spread with butter, brown sugar and cinnamon. Bake at 350° for 10-12 minutes, depending on size.

38

Apple Fritters

JACOB & LORETTA WEAVER

1 egg, beaten
1 c. milk
1 c. peeled & chopped apple
¼ c. sugar
¼ tsp. salt
½ tsp. vanilla
2 c. flour
1 Tbsp. baking powder
3 Tbsp. lemon or orange juice
oil for frying
powdered sugar

Mix dough ingredients together. Drop by teaspoon into hot oil - 350°. Fry until golden brown. Drain on paper towel and roll in powdered sugar. Serve immediately. (Don't make large balls or centers will not be done.) Very yummy!

39

Other Favorite Breads & Rolls

RECIPE FOR _____

_____
_____
_____
_____
_____
_____
_____
_____
_____
_____
_____
_____

RECIPE FOR _____

_____
_____
_____
_____
_____
_____
_____
_____
_____
_____
_____
_____
_____

Breakfast

Fluffy Pancakes

JUSTIN & NAOMI MILLER

2 c. flour
2 c. milk
6 tsp. baking powder
½ tsp. salt
¼ c. sugar
⅓ c. vegetable oil
2 eggs

Mix flour, baking powder, salt and sugar thoroughly. Add rest of ingredients. Serves 8.

Buttermilk Pancakes

MATTHIAS & NAOMI MAST

1 egg
1 c. buttermilk
2 Tbsp. vegetable oil
1 c. flour
1 Tbsp. sugar
½ tsp. baking powder
½ tsp. salt
½ tsp. baking soda

Beat egg, buttermilk and soda. Then add rest of ingredients; beat until smooth. Fry on greased skillet. Yield: 10 (4") pancakes.

42

Oatmeal Pancakes

MATTHEW & MARLENE TROYER

5 c. quick oats
5 Tbsp. maple syrup
4 eggs
½ c. olive oil
2 tsp. baking soda
4 tsp. baking powder

Soak oats in water overnight. (Make sure everything is wet, but no standing water.) Next morning add the rest of ingredients and mix well. Fry on lightly greased hot griddle. We make small (⅓ c.) cakes for easy flipping. Our family's favorite way to serve these is with peanut butter and maple syrup. Serves 8.

Homemade Pancake Batter

JACOB & LORETTA WEAVER

2 c. milk
1 egg
2 tsp. sugar
1 tsp. baking soda
1 tsp. vanilla
½ tsp. salt
2 tsp. baking powder
3 Tbsp. vegetable oil
2 c. flour

Mix first 6 ingredients with egg beater; add last 3 ingredients and mix well. Fry on hot skillet. Serve with syrup. We have made many batches of these fluffy pancakes.

43

Blender Pancakes

SAMUEL & LEANNA WEAVER

1½ c. wheat (whole kernels)
½ c. buckwheat
3 c. milk
4 eggs
1 tsp. salt
⅔ c. vegetable oil
2 Tbsp. honey
2 Tbsp. baking powder

In Bosch blender add wheat, buckwheat and 2 c. milk; mix on speed 4 for 2 minutes. Add final 1 c. milk and blend for additional 2 minutes. Add eggs, vegetable oil, honey and salt. Blend 20 seconds. Add baking powder; blend gently, jogging 'M' switch 3-4 times. (Blender will be full of batter.) Pour batter onto hot griddle or waffle iron. Serves 10.

Pancake Mix

ED & MARY SLABAUGH

5 c. whole wheat flour
3 c. rye flour
2 c. quick oats
1 c. wheat germ
3 c. powdered milk
2 Tbsp. salt
2 Tbsp. + 1 tsp. baking powder

Mix together and store in a tight container in a cool place.

To make pancakes use:
1½ c. mix
2 Tbsp. olive oil
1 egg
water for desired consistency

44

True Belgian Waffles

STEVIE & REBECCA SWAREY

2 c. flour
¾ c. sugar
3½ tsp. baking powder
2 eggs, separated
1½ c. milk
1 c. butter, melted
1 tsp. vanilla

In a bowl, combine flour, sugar and baking powder. In another bowl, lightly beat egg yolks; add milk, butter and vanilla; mix well. Stir into dry ingredients just till combined. Beat egg whites till stiff peaks form. Fold into batter. Bake on waffle pan. Serve with yogurt, strawberries, syrup or vanilla ice cream. Yummy! These waffles get crispy a few minutes off the pan.

Belgian Waffles

SAMUEL & LEANNA WEAVER

2¼ c. unsifted all-purpose flour
½ tsp. salt
2 Tbsp. sugar
1 Tbsp. yeast
1½ c. warm water (125°-130°)
¼ c. melted butter or oil
2 eggs, separated
1 tsp. vanilla

Combine flour, salt, sugar and yeast. Add water, melted butter, egg yolks and vanilla; beat till well combined. Beat egg whites till soft peaks form; fold into batter. Let rise 15 minutes. Heat and grease waffle iron; be sure it's hot enough to make waffles crisp on both sides. Serves 8.

45

French Toast

JACOB & LORETTA WEAVER

6 slices bread or more
2 eggs
1 c. milk
½ c. wheat flour

Mix eggs, milk and flour. Dip bread in egg mixture. Fry on lightly greased skillet. Serve with maple syrup. Delicious!

Baked French Toast

IVAN & BARBARA SCHLABACH

½ lb. butter
1 c. brown sugar
¼ c. maple syrup
12 slices bread
4 oz. cream cheese, softened
cinnamon
6 eggs
1⅔ c. milk
1 tsp. vanilla

Cook first 3 ingredients together till sugar is dissolved. Pour into 10"x15" pan. Spread cream cheese onto 6 pieces of bread. Lay spread side up in pan. Sprinkle with cinnamon. Spread rest of bread with cream cheese and lay spread side down in pan. Sprinkle with cinnamon. Beat last 3 ingredients and pour over top. Refrigerate overnight. Bake at 350°.

46

Creamed Eggs on Toast

MATTHIAS & NAOMI MAST

4 hard-boiled eggs
¼ c. flour
½ tsp. salt
¼ c. butter
2 c. milk
6 slices bacon, fried & crumbled

Fry bacon in skillet; remove and add butter to bacon grease; melt and add flour. Gradually stir in milk, heat until thickened. Add salt, sliced eggs and crumbled bacon. Serve over toast. Serves 3 to 4.

Optional: Add ½ c. Velveeta cheese.

Baked Oatmeal

MATTHIAS & NAOMI MAST

2 eggs
½ c. brown sugar or honey
2 tsp. baking powder
1½ tsp. cinnamon
1 tsp. salt
½ c. vegetable oil or applesauce
1 c. milk
3 c. oatmeal

Bake at 350° for 30-40 minutes. Serve with milk or yogurt.

Note: We like to put a qt. of apple pie filling or blueberries in the pan and top with oatmeal mixture.

Baked Oatmeal

ED & MARY SLABAUGH

½ c. butter, melted
1 c. brown sugar
2 eggs, beaten
3 c. quick oats
2 tsp. baking powder
1 tsp. salt
1 c. milk
1 tsp. vanilla

Cream first 3 ingredients. Add rest of the ingredients and mix and bake in a 10"x10" or 9"x13" pan at 350° for 20-30 minutes. Serves 6 to 8.

Variations: Use ½ c. sugar and add raisins or apples.

47

Pumpkin Grapenuts

MATTHIAS & NAOMI MAST

8 c. whole wheat flour
3 c. brown sugar
1 tsp. salt
1⅓ Tbsp. baking soda
2 tsp. cinnamon
¼ c. applesauce
2 c. milk
3 c. pumpkin
1 tsp. nutmeg

Bake in 2 (9"x13") pans at 350° till done. We grate these and store in freezer. If you like them toasted, toast at 250°, stirring every 15 minutes until crunchy.

Crunchy Granola

JOSIAH & RHODA MILLER

12 c. oatmeal
10 c. Rice Krispies
2 c. coconut
2 pkg. graham crackers, broken
2 c. butter
1½ c. peanut butter
¾ c. water
2½ c. brown sugar
2 tsp. maple flavoring
1½ tsp. salt

Mix first 4 ingredients in large mixing bowl. In a saucepan, combine other ingredients and melt together. Pour over ingredients in bowl and mix well. Put on cookie sheets and toast at 300° for approximately 45 minutes to 1 hour. Stir every 10-15 minutes. Yield: Approx. 2 gallons.

48

Simple and Good Granola

JOHN & ESTA YODER

24 c. oatmeal
4 c. wheat germ
4 c. coconut
3 c. honey
3 c. butter, melted
2 c. chopped nuts (optional)
1 c. flax seeds
4 tsp. vanilla or maple flavoring
  (optional)

Melt butter; add honey and flavoring. Mix dry ingredients together. Add butter and mix well. Bake at 300° for 1 hour or until golden brown.

Granola

JUSTIN & NAOMI MILLER

10 c. rolled oats
4 pkg. graham crackers
4 c. cinnamon crunch cereal
1 tsp. salt
2 tsp. soda
½ c. brown sugar
2 c. butter
½ c. vegetable oil
1 c. honey

Mix first 6 ingredients together. In saucepan melt butter, vegetable oil and honey. Mix together and bake at 300° for 40 minutes. Add 1 c. mini butterscotch chips on top while still hot. For a different flavor add ½ c. peanut butter to butter mixture.

49

Breakfast

Granola

JOSIAH & SUSAN MILLER

20 c. quick oats
2 c. flour
2 pkg. graham crackers, crushed
4 tsp. soda
2 tsp. salt
2 c. honey
2 c. vegetable oil
2 c. butter, melted

Divide into 2 Lifetime roasters. Bake at 300° for approx. 1 hour, stirring every 15 minutes.

Ida Miller Granola

ENOS & NANCY TROYER

14 c. quick oats
2 c. wheat germ
5 c. sweetened coconut
2 pkg. cinnamon graham
crackers, broken
3 c. brown sugar
⅓ c. sesame seed
1 tsp. salt
2 tsp. soda
2 c. butter
1 c. vegetable oil
¼ c. water
1 Tbsp. vanilla
1 Tbsp. maple flavoring

50

Mix together first 8 ingredients. Melt butter; add vegetable oil, water, vanilla and maple flavoring; mix and pour over dry ingredients. Bake at 335° for 12 minutes. Then rotate pans and bake for another 12 minutes; total 24 minutes.

Note: I bake mine a little longer.

Brunch Enchiladas

JOHN & ESTA YODER

2 c. chopped ham
2 c. sausage crumbs
¾ c. chopped onions
¾ c. chopped green peppers
¼ c. butter
16 (8") flour tortillas
16 oz. sour cream
4 c. shredded cheddar cheese
16 eggs
1½ c. milk
2 Tbsp. flour
salt & pepper to taste

Sauté onions and peppers in butter till soft; add meat and cook till hot. Spread a strip of sour cream on each tortilla, add ⅓ c. meat mixture, top with ¼ c. cheese. Roll up and place seams down in 2 (9"x13") pans. Beat the eggs, milk, flour and seasonings together and pour over tortillas. Refrigerate overnight. Remove from fridge 30 minutes before baking. Bake uncovered at 350° for 45 minutes to 1 hour. They're

done once a knife inserted in the center comes out clean. Let set 5 minutes after you have added a thin layer of cheese. Serve with sour cream and salsa. If you only need 1 (9"x13") pan for your family, freeze the other pan and you can thaw it and then bake it.

Note: I like this because you can make it ahead of time and freeze it.

51

Scrambled Eggs

JOSIAH & SUSAN MILLER

1½ c. milk
3 Tbsp. flour, heaping
¾ tsp. baking powder
12 eggs
1 tsp. salt
½ tsp. black pepper

Beat everything together well. These eggs don't get watery or turn green the next day. Serves 14.

Sausage Gravy

JOSIAH & RHODA MILLER

1 lb. pork sausage, mildly
  seasoned
½ c. butter
½ tsp. pepper, scant
1½ tsp. salt
1 tsp. sage (optional)
1¼ c. flour
1½ qt. milk

Brown sausage well, stirring regularly to prevent sticking. Add butter, pepper, salt and sage. When butter bubbles, stir in flour; mix well. Add milk gradually, stirring constantly until thick. Serve hot over biscuits. Makes large skillet full.

Sausage Gravy

MATTHIAS & NAOMI MAST

1 lb. bulk sausage
½-¾ c. flour
milk to desired consistency
salt & pepper to taste

Fry sausage and add flour; add milk to desired consistency. Bring to boil. Add salt and pepper to taste. Serve over eggs and biscuits.

52

Breakfast Casserole

ATLEE & MATTIE MILLER

1½ lb. smokies, cut in 3 pieces
1 layer Tater Tots
sprinkle with seasoning salt
8 eggs, scrambled, fried & salted
shredded Colby cheese
sausage
onions
½ c. sour cream

Fry sausage with onions. Make a gravy. Use a 9"x13" pan. Put smokies on bottom of pan; add in order given. Fry eggs. Add sour cream to sausage gravy. Bake at 350° for 30 minutes.

Breakfast Casserole

JOSEPH & RHODA MILLER

2 lb. sausage
12 eggs
2 lb. Tater Tots
½ c. onions
16 oz. sour cream
2 cans cream of chicken soup
½ tsp. pepper
1 tsp. salt
Velveeta cheese
2 c. cornflake crumbs
½ c. butter

Fry sausage with onion, salt and pepper to taste. Put sausage in bottom of roaster. Fry eggs (keep moist); put on top of sausage. Combine soup, sour cream, salt and pepper; add ¾ c. of milk. Pour over eggs; top with Velveeta cheese. Bake Tater Tots at 350° for 30 minutes while you are putting the rest together. Then put on top of Velveeta cheese. Bake casserole uncovered at 350° for 1 hour. Mix cornflake crumbs with butter and put on top of casserole for the last 15 minutes. Serves 30.

Delicious Breakfast Casserole

JOSIAH & RHODA MILLER

53

1 bag Tater Tots
1 lb. sausage
24 eggs
1 c. milk
1 green pepper
1 med. onion
salt & pepper to taste

Place Tater Tots in small oval roaster. Brown sausage, make into gravy. Put gravy on top of Tater Tots. Beat together eggs and milk. Scramble eggs with pepper and onion that has been sautéed in butter. Add seasonings. Place on top of gravy, cover and bake at 300° until heated through. Before serving, top with Velveeta cheese.

Breakfast Casserole

SAMUEL & LEANNA WEAVER

6 eggs
2 c. milk
2 slices bread, cubed
1 tsp. salt
1 tsp. mustard
½ lb. sausage, browned
½ c. grated cheese
1 c. shredded potatoes

Grease an 8"x12" pan. Put bread in bottom, layer sausage, potatoes and cheese. Beat the rest together and pour over top. Bake at 350° for 45 minutes. Serves 10.

Gold Rush Breakfast Casserole

MICHAEL & JOANNE COBLENTZ

3 c. Tater Tots
2 lb. ham or sausage
12 eggs
1 lb. cheddar cheese

Sauce:
¼ c. butter
¼ c. flour
1¾ c. milk
¼ tsp. salt
pepper to taste
1 c. sour cream

Layer in order given in 9"x13" pan. *For sauce:* Melt butter and add flour and stir. Slowly add milk until it thickens. Remove from heat and add salt, pepper and sour cream. Pour over cheese. Bake at 400° for 30 minutes.

54

Our Favorite Breakfast Casserole

MATTHIAS & NAOMI MAST

home fries
Velveeta cheese
sausage gravy
scrambled eggs with ham &
    mushrooms (optional)
bacon (optional)

Shred and fry potatoes. Put in bottom of casserole dish; top with cheese. Fry sausage and make gravy. Pour over home fries and cheese. Fry ham and mushrooms in a little butter; add beaten eggs and fry. Put on top of sausage gravy and top with more cheese and crumbled bacon.

Breakfast Stacks

MATTHIAS & NAOMI MAST

biscuits
Tater Tots
scrambled eggs
onions
peppers
crumbled bacon
sausage gravy
cheese sauce

Get ingredients for the amount of people you want to serve. Bake biscuits and cut into small pieces. Bake or fry Tater Tots. Scramble eggs. Fry bacon, sauté onions and peppers in bacon grease. Make sausage gravy and prepare cheese sauce. Make stacks on plates in order given.

55

Breakfast

Yogurt

MATTHIAS & NAOMI MAST

1 gal. milk
2 Tbsp. gelatin
cold water
2 c. sugar or cane sugar
4 Tbsp. active yogurt
2 Tbsp. vanilla

Heat milk to 150°. Dissolve gelatin in cold water and stir into milk. Add sugar, yogurt and vanilla. Mix well with wire whisk and set in oven over pilot light overnight or for 8 hours. Add fruit or fruit filling of your choice. Pour into containers and refrigerate. I like to pour it into small containers for the children's lunches.

Yummy Yogurt

STEVIE & REBECCA SWAREY

1 gal. whole milk
2 Tbsp. plain gelatin
½ c. cold water
1¼-1½ c. sugar
4 Tbsp. vanilla
1 c. plain yogurt

Fruit Sauce:
1 c. sugar or less
3-5 c. berries (any berries can be used)

56

Heat milk to 160°. Meanwhile dissolve gelatin in water. Stir into hot milk; cool milk to 130°. (I usually set it in the sink in cold water.) After it reaches 130° add rest of ingredients. Stir well. Set in oven with pilot light for 5 hours or wrap in a towel and set on counter for same length of time. Boil together sugar and fruit for 7 minutes, pour in blender and blend 45 seconds. Chill. When yogurt is done, beat well, add pie filling, beat again. Pour into containers and refrigerate.

Caramel Breakfast Ring

JOSIAH & RHODA MILLER

16 frozen dinner rolls, unbaked
3 oz. pkg. cook-n-serve vanilla
   pudding
pecan pieces
cinnamon

Sauce:
½ c. butter
⅓ c. sugar
⅓ c. brown sugar
¾ c. whipping cream or
   vanilla ice cream

Glaze:
1 c. powdered sugar
2 Tbsp. butter
1 Tbsp. hot milk
pinch of salt

Prepare 3 hours before baking. Spray Bundt pan with cooking spray. Put in a layer of nuts, then put in frozen dinner rolls. Sprinkle with vanilla pudding. Sprinkle cinnamon over the pudding. Mix sauce and pour over rolls. Add another layer of nuts. Cover and let rise until pan is about full. Bake at 325° for 30 minutes. Turn upside down on platter and drizzle with glaze. (This can also be put together before you go to bed and then baked when you get up, but the sauce needs to be cold!)

57

Blueberry Muffins

RICHARD PAUL WEAVER

2 c. flour
1 c. sugar
3 tsp. baking powder
½ tsp. salt
½ c. vegetable oil
2 eggs
1 c. milk
1 c. fresh or frozen blueberries

Mix dry ingredients together. Add vegetable oil, eggs and milk. Fold in blueberries. Bake at 375° for 20-25 minutes. Serves 12.

Blueberry Creme Coffee Cake

MICHAEL & JOANNE COBLENTZ

1 c. sugar
1 c. shortening
1 tsp. soda
1 tsp. baking powder
½ tsp. salt
2 eggs
1 c. sour cream
1 tsp. vanilla
2 c. frozen blueberries
2–2½ c. flour

Crumb Topping:
⅓ c. brown sugar
¼ c. sugar
1 tsp. cinnamon
½ c. nuts or mini chocolate
chips (optional)

Filling:
2 egg whites, beaten
8 oz. cream cheese
2 c. powdered sugar
¼ c. butter
2 tsp. vanilla

Cream together sugar and shortening. Add eggs and beat well. Add remaining ingredients except blueberries. Mix well. Fold in blueberries. Spread batter in greased 9"x13"x2" cake pan or 2 (8") round pans. *For Crumbs:* Mix first 3 ingredients together. Add nuts or chocolate chips or both if desired. Sprinkle over batter. Bake at 350° for 30-35 minutes. Cool. Cut cake in half horizontally. *For Filling:* Combine cream cheese, butter and powdered sugar. Add egg whites and vanilla. Fill coffee cake.

58

Soups and
Vegetables

Taco Soup

MARY LENGACHER

1 lb. ground beef, browned &
   drained
1 sm. onion
1½ qt. tomato juice
1 c. sugar or less
1 pt. sweet corn
15 oz. can chili beans
1 pkg. taco seasoning

Cook together. Serve with corn chips, grated cheese and/or sour cream.

Country Potato Soup

MATTHIAS & NAOMI MAST

3 c. diced, pared potatoes
½ c. carrots
½ c. onion
1½ c. water
2 chicken bouillon cubes
1 tsp. chopped chives
½ tsp. salt
1 c. sour cream
2 Tbsp. flour
2 c. milk

Combine potatoes, carrots, onion, water, bouillon cubes and salt in large saucepan. Cover and cook for about 20 minutes or until potatoes are tender but not mushy. Add 1 c. milk, heat. Mix sour cream, flour, chives and remaining milk in medium bowl. Stir mixture into soup base gradually. Cook over low heat, stirring constantly, until thickened. Add a little Velveeta cheese for extra flavor.

Pizza Soup

JOSEPH & RHODA MILLER

1 lb. sausage
¼ c. chopped onions
¼ c. chopped peppers
2 qt. pizza sauce
4 c. water
6 oz. pkg. pepperoni, cut up
pizza seasoning to taste

Brown onions and peppers with sausage. Add rest of ingredients and simmer. Serves 12.

Cheeseburger Soup

MARY LENGACHER

2 lb. hamburger, browned
4 c. cooked rice
1 c. diced carrots
1 onion, chopped
½ c. diced celery
1 lb. Velveeta cheese
4 c. milk
4 tsp. chicken base seasoning
16 oz. sour cream
salt & pepper to taste

Cook onions, carrots and celery until tender. Add fried hamburger, rice, milk, cheese and seasonings. Mix together and bring to a boil. Add sour cream. Do not boil after adding sour cream.

61

Soups & Vegetables

Chicken Chowder Soup

JOHN & ESTA YODER

2 c. chopped celery
2 c. chopped carrots
2 c. chopped potatoes
½ c. butter
1 tsp. salt
4 c. chicken broth
4 c. milk
¾ c. flour
3-4 c. cooked & diced chicken
2 c. Velveeta cheese

Combine first 6 ingredients; cook until vegetables are soft. Mix flour into half of the milk. Add the rest of milk to vegetables and slowly stir flour and milk mixture into vegetables and cook until thickened. Add cooked chicken and cheese.

Taco Soup

IVAN & BARBARA SCHLABACH

3 qt. tomato juice
2 c. water
¾ c. ketchup
½ c. barbecue sauce
1 onion, chopped
1 Tbsp. salt
1½ Tbsp. chili powder
¾ c. brown sugar
1½ Tbsp. taco seasoning
2 lb. fried hamburger
beans
¾ c. flour

Stir together and heat first 9 ingredients. Thicken with flour and water. Add hamburger and beans.

62

Chili Soup

STEVIE & REBECCA SWAREY

2½ lb. hamburger, browned
½ c. flour
2 qt. tomato juice
1 qt. kidney or pinto beans
1¾ c. brown sugar
½ pkg. chili seasoning
¼ qt. water
¾ c. diced onion
1 pt. ketchup
⅛ c. salt
½ Tbsp. pepper
¼ Tbsp. chili powder

After hamburger is browned add the flour. Mix together all ingredients together and bring to boil.

Celery Soup

STEVIE & REBECCA SWAREY

3 Tbsp. butter
4 c. diced celery & leaves
1 c. leeks or onions
4 c. chicken broth
½ tsp. basil (optional)
2 Tbsp. flour
1 c. milk
1 tsp. salt
¼ tsp. pepper
1 Tbsp. chopped pepper

Sauté celery and onions in butter for 5-8 minutes in a 3 qt. kettle. Add basil, broth, salt, pepper and green pepper and simmer 10-15 minutes or until celery is tender. Blend together flour and milk; add to soup, stirring constantly, until it thickens.

For variations: You can also add shredded carrots and potatoes, if desired; also Velveeta cheese.

63

Soups & Vegetables

Cream of Soup Substitute

MATTHIAS & NAOMI MAST

1½ qt. milk, heated
¾ c. flour
1¼ c. milk
1 Tbsp. Worcestershire sauce
½ tsp. onion salt
½ tsp. celery salt
½ tsp. garlic salt
1 tsp. seasoning salt
¼-½ lb. Velveeta cheese (optional)

Mix flour with 1¼ c. milk; add to hot milk to thicken. Remove from heat and add rest of ingredients. Substitute in recipes calling for soup.

Tramp Soup

MICHAEL & JOANNE COBLENTZ

2 c. diced potatoes
½ lb. sausage
2 qt. milk, divided
½ c. chopped onions
½ c. butter
½ c. flour
1 tsp. salt
⅛ tsp. pepper

Cook and salt potatoes. Brown sausage. In a 3 qt. kettle, melt butter and brown onions, then add flour and cook for 1 minute, stirring. Add 1 qt. milk, stirring often until boiling. Add 1 qt. heated milk, potatoes and sausage.

64

Honey-Glazed Carrots

MATTHIAS & NAOMI MAST

1¼ lb. carrots
3 Tbsp. butter
2 Tbsp. honey
1 Tbsp. brown sugar or
   maple syrup

Cook carrots in water with salt till soft. Melt butter in skillet. Stir in honey and brown sugar. Cook and stir for 2 minutes or until thickened and bubbly. Add carrots and toss gently. Serves 4 to 6.

Salads and
Salad Dressings

Cole Slaw

VERNON & RUTH YODER

1 head cabbage, shredded
1 head broccoli, cut in pieces
2 carrots, shredded
1 onion, chopped
1 pepper, diced
1 lb. bacon, crisply fried
8 oz. shredded cheese

Place shredded cabbage onto large serving plate. Add broccoli, carrots, onions and pepper in layers. Pour dressing on top. Put bacon and cheese on top of dressing.

Dressing:
2 c. salad dressing (Miracle Whip)
1 c. sugar
1 tsp. salt
1 tsp. vinegar
2 tsp. celery seed

Kline Cousin Cole Slaw Favorite

ATLEE & MATTIE MILLER

66

1 lg. cabbage, shredded
1 sm. onion, chopped
1 c. sour cream
1 c. Miracle Whip
1 c. sugar
1 tsp. salt
1 tsp. celery seed

Mix dressing together and stir into cabbage. Top with bacon crumbles and shredded cheese. Very simple and creamy. Serves lots. Enjoy!

Olive Garden Layer Salad

JOSIAH & RHODA MILLER

1½ bunches romaine lettuce
¾ c. carrots
⅔ c. sliced banana peppers
black olives, sliced
2 c. shredded mozzarella cheese
1 c. chopped tomatoes
croutons

Layer ingredients in order given. Serve with ranch and Italian dressing. Serves 8 to 10.

Summer Salad

JOSIAH & RHODA MILLER

1 med. cucumber, sliced thin
2 med. yellow summer squash, sliced thin
2 med. tomatoes, sliced (paste tomatoes are nice to use)
Vidalia sweet onion, sliced

Arrange cucumbers, squash, tomatoes and onions on a serving platter. Pour dressing over top and sprinkle with garlic salt. Refrigerate until ready to serve. Serves 6 to 8.

A very colorful salad and delicious!

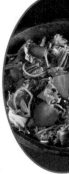

67

Dressing:
¼ c. vegetable oil
1 tsp. dried basil
2 Tbsp. lemon juice

2 Tbsp. apple cider vinegar
1 tsp. sugar
¼ tsp. salt

Salads & Salad Dressings

Crunchy Tossed Salad

LUKE & KATHRYN MILLER

1 lg. head lettuce
8 bacon strips
⅓ c. sliced almonds, toasted
¼ c. sesame seeds, toasted
4 green onions, sliced
¾ c. chow mein noodles
sunflower seeds (optional)

Mix all together just before serving. Sprinkle noodles on top.

Dressing:
½ c. vegetable oil
¼ c. sugar
2 Tbsp. vinegar

1 tsp. salt
¼ tsp. pepper

Strawberry Bacon Spinach Salad

JOSIAH & RHODA MILLER

1 (6 oz.) pkg. spinach
1 pt. fresh strawberries, sliced
8 bacon strips, cooked & crumbled
¼ c. chopped red onion
¼ c. chopped walnuts

In medium-sized bowl, combine spinach, strawberries, bacon, onions and walnuts. Pour dressing over salad just before serving. Serves 6 to 8.

Dressing:
1 c. mayonnaise
½ c. sugar

¼ c. raspberry vinegar

68

Strawberry Crunch Salad

MATTHEW & MARLENE TROYER

2-3 heads leaf lettuce
2 c. shredded mozzarella cheese
¾ qt. strawberries
4 c. chow mein noodles
¾ c. pecans
¾ c. vegetable oil
1 c. sugar
⅓ c. vinegar
2 tsp. poppy seeds
1 tsp. salt
1 tsp. pepper
2 Tbsp. sour cream, rounded

For Dressing: Cook vegetable oil, sugar and vinegar for 1 minute. Add poppy seeds, salt, pepper and sour cream. Cool completely. When ready to serve, mix dressing with rest of ingredients. This fills a fix-n-mix bowl.

Oriental Salad

JOHN & ESTA YODER

1 bunch romaine lettuce
½ c. diced green onions
1 pkg. crumbled ramen noodles, chicken flavored
½ c. sliced almonds
2 Tbsp. sesame seeds

Dressing:
4 Tbsp. sugar
½ c. vegetable oil
6 Tbsp. red wine vinegar
1 tsp. pepper
flavor packet

Shred lettuce and add diced onions. Toast noodles, almonds and sesame seeds in butter; cool and add to lettuce. Shake dressing ingredients in a jar 10 minutes before serving. Mix with salad.

Optional: Grilled chicken pieces or crumbled bacon makes this extra good!

69

Salads & Salad Dressings

Cauliflower Salad

STEVE & MIRIAM LENGACHER

1 head lettuce
10 oz. frozen peas
1 med. onion
4 oz. cheddar cheese
2 pkg. bacon, fried
1 head cauliflower

Dressing:
2 c. salad dressing
2 Tbsp. sugar

½ tsp. salt

Pour dressing on top of salad, then set in refrigerator overnight. Stir in the morning.

Broccoli Slaw

JOSEPH & RHODA MILLER

1 lg. bunch broccoli
1 bunch green onions
1 red pepper
1 c. sunflower seeds
1 c. sliced almonds
1 pkg. ramen noodles
¾ c. bacon crumbles
1 c. shredded cheddar cheese

Dressing:
¾ c. vegetable oil
½ c. sugar

⅓ c. red wine vinegar
1½ Tbsp. chicken base

Cut broccoli in small pieces. Slice green onions and cut peppers in small pieces. Brown sunflower seeds, almonds and ramen noodles in butter. Mix just before serving. Serves 10. *For Dressing:* Simmer to dissolve.

70

Colorful Romaine Salad

MATTHIAS & NAOMI MAST

1 head romaine lettuce
1 head broccoli
green onion
1 green pepper
1 red pepper
2 Tbsp. butter or bacon grease
2 pkg. ramen noodles, crushed
1 c. pecans or slivered almonds

Dressing:
1 c. vegetable oil
1 Tbsp. soy sauce
¼ tsp. salt

¼ tsp. pepper
½ c. vinegar
1 c. sugar

Cut up first 5 ingredients and mix together. Fry ramen noodles and pecans or slivered almonds in butter or bacon grease. Cool and add to cut-up lettuce. *For Dressing:* Heat vinegar and sugar to melt, then add vegetable oil, soy sauce, salt and pepper.

Simple Salad

MATTHIAS & NAOMI MAST

1 head lettuce
2 c. cheese
2 c. croutons

Dressing:
1 c. Miracle Whip
1 c. sugar
½ c. vinegar

1 tsp. celery salt
¾ c. vegetable oil

71

Salads & Salad Dressings

Dorothy's Chinese Cole Slaw

MATTHIAS & NAOMI MAST

1 med. head cabbage
1 c. almonds
2 pkg. ramen noodles
green onions (optional)
4 Tbsp. butter

Dressing:
⅓ c. vinegar
1 c. cane sugar
¼ tsp. salt

¼ tsp. pepper
1 c. vegetable oil
seasoning from noodles

Shred cabbage and place in bowl. Melt 2 Tbsp. butter and toast almonds and crushed ramen noodles. Mix dressing ingredients, stir all together and serve.

Overnight Salad

JAMES & IDA LEHMAN

1 lg. head lettuce, chopped
1 sm. onion, chopped
1 sm. head cauliflower, chopped
1 lb. bacon, fried & crumbled
1½ c. shredded cheese

Dressing:
1½ c. salad dressing
¼ c. sugar
⅓ c. Parmesan cheese

Use a 9"x13" Tupperware pan. Layer ingredients in order given, except cheese. Put dressing on top. Spread evenly. Sprinkle cheese on top. Keep refrigerated till ready to serve. Toss salad just before serving. Serves 16.

72

Bacon Chicken Salad

MATTHIAS & NAOMI MAST

2 heads lettuce
4 hard-boiled eggs
20 pcs. bacon
2-3 lb. chicken
cheddar cheese

Dressing:
1¼ c. Miracle Whip
⅔ c. barbecue sauce
2 Tbsp. lemon juice
5 Tbsp. sugar
1 tsp. salt
½ tsp. pepper
½ tsp. Liquid Smoke

Chicken Salad

IVAN & BARBARA SCHLABACH

1 head lettuce
2 c. chow mein noodles
½ c. almonds
1 (20 oz.) can crushed pineapple,
    drained
onion
green pepper
sunflower seeds
2 c. marinated chicken, grilled

Dressing:
2 Tbsp. Miracle Whip
1 c. vegetable oil
¼ c. water
1 c. sugar
¼ c. vinegar
½ tsp. pepper
1 tsp. salt
½ tsp. poppy seed
1 tsp. celery seed
1 Tbsp. Worcestershire sauce
2 tsp. mustard

Stir together dressing ingredients
and mix with lettuce mixture.

73

Salads & Salad Dressings

Oriental Chicken Salad

JOSIAH & SUSAN MILLER

1 head romaine lettuce
1 lb. grilled chicken
1-2 peppers
1 sm. onion
almonds
ramen noodles

Sauté almonds and ramen noodles. Cut up rest of ingredients.

Dressing:
½ c. sugar
½ c. vegetable oil
¼ c. vinegar

1 tsp. poppy seeds (optional)
½ tsp. salt
½ tsp. pepper

Taco Salad Dressing

JOSIAH & SUSAN MILLER

1½ c. vegetable oil
½ c. tomato juice
½ c. vinegar
2 c. Sucanat or brown sugar
4 Tbsp. mayonnaise
2 Tbsp. taco seasoning mix
4 tsp. mustard
1½ c. kidney beans, cooked, or
   1 (15.5 oz.) can, drained

Put all ingredients in blender and blend on high speed till smooth.

Corn Chip Salad

MICHAEL & JOANNE COBLENTZ

1 head lettuce
6 eggs
1 lb. bacon
½ lb. cheddar cheese
5 c. corn chips

Mix everything together just before serving.

Dressing:
1 c. salad dressing
⅛ c. vinegar
¼ c. milk

¼ c. sugar
¼ c. brown sugar

Corn Chip Salad

MATTHEW & MARLENE TROYER

2 heads leaf lettuce
1 lb. bacon
¾ lb. cheese, shredded
8 hard-boiled eggs
6-8 c. corn chips

Mix dressing ingredients beforehand. Prepare salad ingredients and mix everything together when ready to serve. This will fill a Tupperware fix-n-mix bowl.

Dressing:
2 c. mayonnaise
⅛ c. vinegar
½ c. water

½ c. sugar
½ c. brown sugar

75

Salads & Salad Dressings

Frito Salad

JAY & AMY TROYER

1 can beans
1 bag corn chips, crushed
1 (16 oz.) bag shredded cheese
1 head lettuce, shredded
1 pkg. of 3 heads romaine
    lettuce, shredded

Toss together salad ingredients with dressing in fix-n-mix bowl.

Dressing:

2 c. salad dressing
1½ c. sugar
¼ c. vinegar
½ c. vegetable oil

2 tsp. mustard
4 tsp. water
1 tsp. paprika
½ tsp. salt

Frito Salad

IVAN & BARBARA SCHLABACH

1 can beans
1 bag corn chips
16 oz. shredded cheese
1 head lettuce
1 pkg. romaine lettuce

Dressing:

2 c. salad dressing
1½ c. sugar
¼ c. vinegar
½ c. ketchup
2 tsp. mustard
4 tsp. water
1 tsp. paprika
½ tsp. salt
½ c. vegetable oil

Pasta Salad

MARY LENGACHER

1 (12 oz.) box tri-colored
   pasta twists
carrots
broccoli
onion
green pepper
tomato
2 c. diced ham
shredded cheese

Dressing:
1 c. salad dressing
¼ c. sugar
4 tsp. vinegar

Cook pasta till soft; drain and cool. Parboil carrots and broccoli, any amount. Cool. Chop onion, green pepper, tomatoes, any amount. Add vegetables and ham to pasta, and also shredded cheese. Then stir in dressing.

½ tsp. dill weed, scant
½ tsp. salt

Pasta Salad

MATTHIAS & NAOMI MAST

1½ lb. pasta
¾ lb. cheddar cheese, cubed
1 lb. ham, cubed
1 green pepper
1 red pepper
bacon

Dressing:
3 c. Miracle Whip
¼ c. mustard
½ tsp. salt
1½ c. sugar

Cook pasta until tender; rinse immediately with cold water, then add cheese, ham, peppers and bacon.

Be creative and add vegetables of your choice. I have added cucumbers and tomatoes.

¾ c. vegetable oil
½ c. vinegar
1 Tbsp. onion salt
½ Tbsp. celery seed

Salads & Salad Dressings

Pasta Salad

JOHN & ESTA YODER

1 box spiral pasta
1 sm. onion, chopped
1 med. green pepper, chopped
1 c. diced carrots
3-6 hard-boiled eggs, chopped
crumbled bacon
2 c. shredded cheddar cheese

Cook pasta; drain and rinse with cold water. When cool add rest of ingredients. Mix all dressing ingredients and add to pasta. Refrigerate before serving.

Dressing:
3 c. Miracle Whip
¾ c. sour cream
2 tsp. salt

6 tsp. mustard
2 c. sugar

Pasta Salad

IVAN & BARBARA SCHLABACH

1½ lb. noodles
8 oz. diced ham
diced tomatoes
diced onions
diced green peppers
1½ c. cheddar cheese
bacon

Cook noodles just until soft. Drain and add ham, tomatoes, onions, peppers, cheese and bacon. Stir together dressing ingredients and add to noodles. Yield: 1 gal.

Dressing:
3 c. Miracle Whip
¼ c. spicy brown mustard
¾ c. vegetable oil
¼ c. vinegar
1½ c. sugar

½ Tbsp. celery seed
½ tsp. salt
dash onion salt
¼ c. Italian dressing

78

Pasta Salad

JAMES & IDA LEHMAN

1½ lb. macaroni
10 oz. cubed ham
1 c. chopped celery
1 c. cherry tomatoes
1 sm. onion, chopped
½ c. chopped green peppers
2 c. shredded cheese

Mix dressing ingredients and pour over pasta mixture. Refrigerate and serve. Serves 25.

Dressing:
3 c. salad dressing
⅓ c. mustard
½ c. vegetable oil
1 tsp. onion salt

¼ c. vinegar
1½ c. sugar
1 Tbsp. salt
½ Tbsp. celery seeds

Cornbread Salad

MATTHEW & MARLENE TROYER

2 (8½ oz.) pkg. cornbread mix
¼ tsp. cumin
¼ tsp. oregano
2 Tbsp. ranch dressing mix
2 c. sour cream
2 c. mayonnaise
4 tomatoes, diced
1½ c. diced peppers
2 (15 oz.) cans pinto beans
1 lb. bacon, fried & crumbled
4 c. shredded cheese

Bake cornbread according to directions. Mix in cumin and oregano; then bake at 375° in a 9"x13" pan. Combine mayonnaise, dressing mix and sour cream. Crumble half of cornbread into large rectangle Tupperware cake taker. Add half of rest of ingredients on top. Repeat layers. Cover and refrigerate till ready to serve. Serves 30 to 35.

79

Cornbread Salad

JOHN & ESTA YODER

1½ c. flour
1½ c. cornmeal
½ tsp. salt
⅓ c. honey
3 eggs
⅛ tsp. onion powder
¼ tsp. baking powder
¼ c. butter
⅛ tsp. oregano
½ c. salsa
1 c. milk with 2 tsp. soda
1 tsp. vinegar

Dressing:
1 c. mayonnnaise
1 c. sour cream

½ pkg. dry ranch mix

Mix and bake in 9"x13" pan. Cool. Crumble in a dish. Layer with diced green pepper, chopped tomatoes, diced sweet onion, canned beans of your choice and whole kernel corn, drained, and shredded cheddar cheese. Drizzle dressing over this and layer again, starting with cornbread.

Potato Salad

MICHAEL & JOANNE COBLENTZ

12 c. potatoes, cooked & shredded
12 hard-boiled eggs
1 c. chopped onions
1½ c. chopped celery

Dressing:
3 c. salad dressing
3 Tbsp. vinegar
3 Tbsp. mustard

4 tsp. salt
2 c. sugar
½ c. milk

Shred potatoes and eggs. Add onions and celery. Mix dressing and add to potatoes. Yield: 1 gal. Serves 20.

Potato Salad

6 c. cooked potatoes, diced or
   shredded
6 hard-boiled eggs, diced
½ c. finely chopped celery
1 Tbsp. finely chopped onions

Dressing:
1½ c. salad dressing
2 Tbsp. mustard or less
⅛ c. vinegar

1 c. sugar
1¾ tsp. salt
¼ c. milk, scant

Mix dressing ingredients together and pour over potato mixture. Refrigerate. Yield: ½ gal.

Potato Salad

12 c. cooked potatoes
12 eggs
1 c. celery
1 med. onion
¼ c. mustard
¼ c. vinegar
2 c. salad dressing
½ c. milk
2 tsp. salt
1 c. sugar

LARRY & NAOMI LENGACHER

Shred potatoes, eggs and onion; mix together while warm, as this adds a better flavor to the salad. Add celery. Mix salad dressing, sugar, milk, vinegar, mustard and salt. Add to potato mixture.

81

Potato Salad

ATLEE & MATTIE MILLER

12 c. cooked & shredded
  potatoes
10 hard-boiled eggs
1 sm. onion, chopped fine
2 c. diced celery

Dressing:
3 c. Miracle Whip
¼ c. vinegar
4 tsp. salt

Cook and shred potatoes. Peel eggs and shred. Whip dressing together; add onions and celery and pour over potatoes and eggs. Best if set overnight before serving. Serves 25 to 30. Yield: 1 gal.

¼ c. mustard
2½ c. sugar

Delicious Bean Salad

JOSIAH & SUSAN MILLER

1 qt. green beans
1 qt. cooked carrots
1 can kidney beans
2 c. celery (optional)
1 onion
cauliflower (optional)

Mix dressing together, then add to vegetables.

Dressing:
1 c. sugar
1 tsp. salt
½ tsp. pepper
1 tsp. celery seed

3 tsp. mustard
⅓ c. vinegar
1 c. vegetable oil
2 Tbsp. Miracle Whip

82

Gourmet Eggs

MATTHIAS & NAOMI MAST

3 Tbsp. Miracle Whip
2 tsp. sugar
2 dashes salt and pepper
2 tsp. vinegar
2 dashes Worcestershire sauce
2 tsp. mustard
12 eggs

Place eggs in saucepan; cover with water and boil for 15 minutes. Cool eggs in cold water. Crack and peel eggs, cut in ½ lengthwise and remove yolks. Mash yolks and combine with other ingredients, beating until smooth. Refill egg whites with egg yolk mixture. Garnish with paprika.

Clear Salad Dressing

MARCUS & ROSANNA MAST

1 c. sugar
1 c. vegetable oil
¼ c. vinegar
2 tsp. mustard
2 Tbsp. Miracle Whip
1 tsp. salt
¼ tsp. black pepper
1 Tbsp. Worcestershire sauce
1 tsp. onion salt

Mix everything together.

83

Sweet and Sour Dressing

JACOB & LORETTA WEAVER

4 c. Miracle Whip
2 c. sugar
¼ c. mustard or less
a little celery seed or celery salt

Dressing for lettuce salad.

Salads & Salad Dressings

Sweet and Sour Dressing

MARY LENGACHER

1 c. sugar
¼ c. vinegar
½ tsp. celery seed
5 Tbsp. salad dressing
1 sm. onion, cut fine
1 tsp. salt
¼ tsp. black pepper
3 tsp. prepared mustard
1 c. vegetable oil

Place all ingredients in blender except oil and blend slowly. Add oil and mix well.

Slaw Dressing

JACOB & LORETTA WEAVER

12 c. salad dressing/Miracle Whip
1 c. vinegar
1 c. mustard
8 c. sugar
½ c. milk
3 Tbsp. salt

Can also be used for potato or pasta salad dressing.

84

Dressing for Cabbage

MATTHIAS & NAOMI MAST

¾ c. salad dressing
¼ c. mustard
½ tsp. celery seed
½ c. vinegar
½ c. vegetable oil
1 tsp. onion salt
1½ c. sugar
8 oz. cream cheese
⅔ c. milk

Use 1 c. dressing to 1 qt. cabbage. Beat cream cheese (room temp.); add sugar and beat until smooth; add remaining ingredients.

French Dressing

MATTHIAS & NAOMI MAST

¾ c. water
1 c. vinegar
4 c. ketchup
2 c. vegetable oil
2 Tbsp. salt
2 Tbsp. celery seed
2 Tbsp. paprika
8 c. sugar

Combine all ingredients and mix to dissolve sugar.

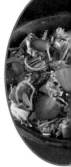

85

Salads & Salad Dressings

French Dressing

JOSIAH & RHODA MILLER

1 c. sugar
1 c. Wesson oil
½ c. ketchup*
2 Tbsp. vinegar
1 tsp. Worcestershire sauce
½ c. salad dressing
pinch of salt

Put all ingredients in blender and blend. *When using homemade ketchup I use a good ⅔ c.

Homemade Miracle Whip

MATTHIAS & NAOMI MAST

2 eggs & water to make ¾ c.
1 Tbsp. lemon juice
2 tsp. salt
⅔ c. cane sugar
⅓ c. honey
½ tsp. mustard
¾ c. vegetable oil

Combine ingredients in blender. In saucepan, combine ⅔ c. wheat flour, 1 c. water and ⅓ c. vinegar. Bring to a boil and add to blender and blend until smooth. If your family doesn't like it on sandwiches, try it in lettuce dressing.

86

Homemade Croutons

MARCUS & ROSANNA MAST

1 loaf bread, cut up in sm. cubes
½ c. butter, melted
seasoned salt
garlic salt
onion salt

Layer bread on large cookie sheet, drizzle with butter and sprinkle with seasoned salt, garlic salt and onion salt. Mix together and bake at 250° for 1 hour or till desired crunchiness. Stir frequently.

Homemade Croutons

JOSIAH & RHODA MILLER

2 Tbsp. butter, melted
1 Tbsp. olive oil
¼ tsp. garlic powder
¼ tsp. onion powder
¼ tsp. dried oregano
¼ tsp. dried basil
6 slices day-old bread, cubed

Put together and bake at 300° for 20-25 minutes or until a little crisp.

87

Salads & Salad Dressings

RECIPE FOR _____

_____
_____
_____
_____
_____
_____
_____
_____
_____
_____
_____
_____
_____

RECIPE FOR _____

_____
_____
_____
_____
_____
_____
_____
_____
_____
_____
_____
_____
_____

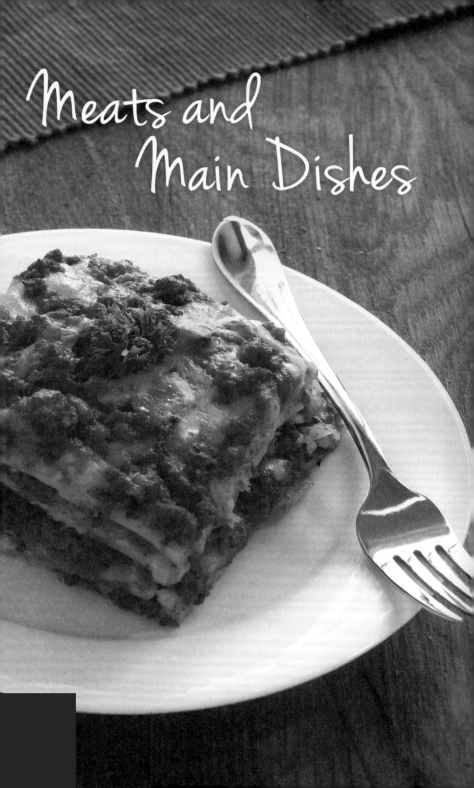

Meats and Main Dishes

Herb Potatoes

JOSIAH & SUSAN MILLER

7 lb. potatoes
1 c. butter
1½ Tbsp. garlic salt
1½ Tbsp. parsley
1 Tbsp. minced onion
¼ Tbsp. salt
¼ Tbsp. pepper

Bake at 350° for 3 hours. Feeds a little more than a family of 10. Serves approx. 15 adults.

Potato Stack Casserole

MATTHIAS & NAOMI MAST

10 lb. potatoes, cooked & diced
2½ c. sour cream
2½ c. milk
2 pkg. ranch dressing mix
salt & pepper to taste
4 lb. hamburger, fried, and add
    2 pkg. taco seasoning

90

Cook and dice potatoes then add sour cream, milk, ranch dressing, salt and pepper. Layer potato mixture in dish; top with hamburger. Heat. Make 3 qt. of your favorite cheese sauce and put on top just before serving. Crush 1 bag taco chips and sprinkle on top of cheese sauce.

Oven-Fried Potatoes

ENOS & NANCY TROYER

8 lg. baking potatoes, unpeeled
½ c. olive oil
4 Tbsp. Parmesan cheese
1 tsp. salt
½ tsp. garlic powder
½ tsp. paprika
¼ tsp. pepper
a dash of cayenne pepper

Cut potatoes in 4 wedges lengthwise. Place skin side down in pan. Combine remaining ingredients; brush over potatoes. Bake at 375° for 1 hour, brushing with cheese mixture at 15-minute intervals. Turn potatoes over for last 15 minutes. These are wonderful with any roasted meat or fine as a snack. Serves 6 to 8.

Gourmet Potatoes

MATTHEW & MARLENE TROYER

10 lb. potatoes, cooked & mashed
1½ lb. sour cream
1 Tbsp. minced onion
¾ c. butter
2 cans evaporated milk
salt to taste
3 c. cheddar cheese

Mix (beat) all ingredients together. If it's too stiff, add milk. Brown butter and put on top when done. This can be made ahead of time. Serves 20 to 25.

91

Meats & Main Dishes

Scrumptious Outdoor Kettle Potatoes

ATLEE & MATTIE MILLER

1 lb. bacon, cut in pieces
1 med. onion, thin sliced
8 lg. potatoes with skins
1½ c. Sierra Mist
2 tsp. salt
2 tsp. garlic with parsley
2 tsp. Lawry's salt
2 tsp. Nature's salt
½ lb. cheddar, grated, or
   Velveeta cheese slices

Brown bacon in kettle; add onions; cook till crisp. Put potatoes through coarse Salad Master. Put potatoes, bacon and onions. In kettle, add Sierra Mist and seasonings, stir a few times and keep lid on. When done, add cheese. I stir before serving. Serves 10.

Mashed Potato Balls

VERNON & RUTH YODER

2 c. stiff mashed potatoes
2 c. chopped ham
1 c. shredded Swiss cheese
⅓ c. Miracle Whip
¼ c. minced onion
1 egg, well beaten
1 tsp. prepared mustard
½ tsp. salt
¼ tsp. pepper

Mix all together and form into balls. Roll in 3½ c. cornflake crumbs. Bake at 350° for 30 minutes. Yield: 4 doz.

92

Quick Tater Bake

MATTHIAS & NAOMI MAST

2 lb. hamburger
8 oz. cream cheese
1 c. ketchup
1 c. milk
1 can cream of mushroom soup
1 bag Tater Tots, divided
Velveeta cheese

Fry hamburger; stir in cream cheese, ketchup, milk and soup. Add ½ of Tater Tots, top with cheese and bake at 325° for 45 minutes. Put rest of Tater Tots on top and bake 30 minutes longer to brown Tater Tots. This recipe x4 fills an electric roaster.

Tater Tot Casserole

VERNON & RUTH YODER

1 pt. sour cream
2 cans cream of chicken soup
½ soup can milk
½ c. chopped onion
½ lb. Velveeta cheese
2 lb. Tater Tots
2 lb. hamburger
½ lb. Velveeta cheese, sliced
2 c. cornflake crumbs
½ c. butter

Brown hamburger; add salt and pepper; set aside. Put Tater Tots in casserole dish. Heat sour cream, cream of chicken soup, milk, onions and cheese. Stir occasionally. When cheese is melted, pour over Tater Tots. Sprinkle hamburger over top. Place sliced Velveeta cheese on hamburger. Bake at 350° for ½-¾ hour covered, then uncover and add cornflake crumbs, mixed with butter. Bake uncovered for ½ hour.

93

Meats & Main Dishes

Hot Potato Salad

LUKE & KATHRYN MILLER

5 lb. potatoes
½ lb. Velveeta cheese
1 tsp. prepared mustard
1 lg. onion, chopped
1½ c. Miracle Whip
¾ c. milk
salt & pepper to taste
bacon, cut in squares

Cook, cool and shred potatoes. Combine all in casserole, except bacon. Top with uncooked bacon. Bake at 350° till bacon is done.

Underground Ham Casserole

JACOB & LORETTA WEAVER

4 Tbsp. butter
½ c. diced onion
1 Tbsp. Worcestershire sauce
4 c. ham, cubed
2 c. Velveeta cheese
2 cans cream of mushroom soup
1 c. milk
4 qt. mashed potatoes
1 pt. sour cream
1 lb. bacon, fried & crumbled

Cook first 4 ingredients until onions are tender. Place in bottom of roaster, heat next 3 ingredients until cheese is melted. Put on top of first layer. Mash the potatoes, mixing with sour cream. Spread on second layer and put bacon on top. Bake at 325° until heated through.

Sweet Potato Pie Casserole

LUKE & KATHRYN MILLER

2 c. cooked sweet potatoes
⅓ c. butter
½ c. sugar
½ tsp. salt
2 eggs
1 tsp. vanilla
2 tsp. flour

Beat together eggs, vanilla and flour. Add butter, sweet potatoes, sugar and salt; mix well. Put in 9"x9" pan. Put crumbs on top and bake at 350° for 35 minutes.

Crumbs:
⅓ c. flour, rounded
1 c. chopped pecans

¼ c. butter
¾ c. brown sugar

Sweet Potato Casserole

JUSTIN & NAOMI MILLER

2 c. cooked sweet potatoes
⅓ c. butter
½ c. sugar
½ tsp. salt
2 eggs
1 tsp. vanilla
2 tsp. flour

Mash potatoes. Add butter, sugar and salt. Beat eggs, vanilla and flour; mix thoroughly. Grease casserole dish or 8"x8" pan and pour mixture in. Mix and spread crumbs over potatoes. Bake at 350° for 35 minutes. May be prepared the day before.

Crumbs:
1 c. chopped pecans
⅓ c. flour

2½ Tbsp. butter
½ c. brown sugar

95

Dressing (Stuffing)

MATTHIAS & NAOMI MAST

1 loaf of bread
1 c. carrots
1 c. potatoes
onions to taste
4-5 eggs, beaten
2 c. chicken
2 c. chicken broth
1 Tbsp. chicken base
½ tsp. black pepper
1 tsp. salt
½ tsp. seasoning salt
milk to desired consistency

Toast bread, cut up into small squares. Cook vegetables. Mix all together in large bowl. Fry until golden brown and bake to desired doneness.

Dressing

LARRY & NAOMI LENGACHER

½ c. butter
2 loaves bread
1 qt. milk
4 eggs, beaten
1 pt. cooked chicken
½ pt. diced carrots, cooked
½ pt. diced potatoes, cooked
½ pt. uncooked celery
onions to your taste
½ Tbsp. salt
black pepper
lemon pepper
parsley flakes

Brown bread in pan on stove. Mix rest of ingredients. Mix together and bake at 350° till done. Serve with gravy.

96

Noodles

JOSEPH & RHODA MILLER

1 lb. noodles
7 c. chicken broth
3 Tbsp. chicken base
1½ tsp. salt
3 c. water
10.5 oz. cream of chicken soup
½ c. butter, browned

Heat water, broth, seasonings and soup to boiling; add noodles. Let boil again, then turn off. Brown butter and pour on top; let set for 1 hour before serving. Don't stir till ready to serve. Serves 15.

Chicken Noodles

JOSIAH & RHODA MILLER

5 qt. chicken and broth
water to fill ⅔ full
1 c. chicken base
⅓ c. Lawry's seasoned salt
1 Tbsp. salt
2 tsp. pepper
5 lb. noodles (Inn Maid-med.)
3 cans cream of chicken soup

Bring first 6 ingredients to boiling, then add noodles. Bring to boil again. Let set 20 minutes. Add soup and stir. Let set 1 hour or more. Yield: 1 stock pot.

97

Veggie-Noodle Ham Blend

JOHN & ESTA YODER

12 oz. wide noodles
1 can cream of broccoli soup
1 can cream of chicken soup
2 c. frozen corn, thawed
1½ c. cubed cooked ham
1½ c. California Blend vegetables
1½ c. milk
2 Tbsp. parsley
¼ tsp. salt
½ tsp. pepper
1 c. shredded cheddar cheese

Cook noodles; drain. In a bowl, combine soups and milk. Stir in noodles, corn, vegetables, ham, parsley, pepper, salt and ¾ of cheese. Transfer to a greased 9"x13" pan. Cover and bake at 350° for 45 minutes. Uncover; sprinkle with remaining cheese. Bake 10 minutes longer or until bubbly and cheese is melted.

Table-Long Burrito

MATTHIAS & NAOMI MAST

6 lb. hamburger, fried
2 (30 oz.) cans chili beans
2 pkg. burrito seasoning or
    taco seasoning
2 c. dry rice, prepared
2 heads lettuce, cut fine
2 lb. shredded cheese
4 (10 pk.) burrito shells
tomatoes
  Serve in bowls:
½ gal. cheese sauce
1½ pt. salsa
2 cans olives (optional)
hot peppers (optional)
2 pt. sour cream

Fry hamburger; add beans and seasonings. Prepare rice and cut up lettuce. When ready to serve, warm burritos for 30 minutes at 300°. Place foil through middle of a long table, place warm burritos to one side of the foil, overlapping edges of burritos. Spoon hamburger mixture in the middle of warm burritos; top with rice and cheese. Roll burritos over, folding the edge under. Top with lettuce and tomato. Serve with cheese sauce, sour cream, olives, salsa and peppers. Serve immediately. Serves 24.

Mexican Dish
from Chipotle's Fast Food

ATLEE & MATTIE MILLER

2 c. uncooked rice
1 (2 lb.) can Bush baked beans
16 oz. sour cream
4 lb. diced chicken
1 lg. onion, sliced
2 lg. green peppers
1 qt. salsa
shredded Colby cheese
shredded lettuce

Cook rice as directed, adding 1 Tbsp. Southwest dip mix. Heat beans; sauté chicken in Italian dressing plus salt to taste. Sauté onions and peppers till soft. Serve in order given. Serves 10. Enjoy!

Chicken Haystacks

JOSIAH & SUSAN MILLER

2 c. rice
1 c. chopped celery
½ c. chopped onion
1-2 lb. chicken breasts
4 peppers
2 lg. onions

Sauté rice, celery and onion until lightly browned in ¼ c. butter. Season with Nature's seasoning and cook with 4 c. chicken broth, 1 tsp. Worcestershire sauce, 1 tsp. soy sauce, 1 tsp. dried oregano and 1 tsp. thyme. Sauté peppers and onions in butter. Sauté chicken slivers and season with garlic salt and Lawry's seasoning salt. *Haystack order:* rice, chicken, lettuce, salsa, shredded Mexican cheese, ranch dressing.

99

Chicken Stir-Fry

JOSIAH & SUSAN MILLER

⅔ c. Italian dressing
1 lg. onion
3 c. carrots
1 qt. beans
1 qt. chicken broth
1 Tbsp. garlic salt
2 tsp. salt
1 Tbsp. soy sauce
1-2 lb. chicken breasts

In skillet fry chicken breasts, cut into bite size pieces with Italian dressing and oil. Season with garlic salt and seasoning salt. Add onions and carrots, cut into slivers and simmer until soft. Add rest of ingredients and thicken a little with clear jel. Serve over rice.

Chickenetti

MATTHIAS & NAOMI MAST

100

8 oz. spaghetti
1 Tbsp. vegetable oil
2 Tbsp. chopped onion
3 Tbsp. butter
1 Tbsp. flour
1 c. chicken broth
1 tsp. salt
1 tsp. Lawry's seasoned salt
1 tsp. garlic salt
1 c. milk
1 can cream of chicken soup
1 c. Velveeta cheese
2 Tbsp. parsley
3 c. diced chicken
1 c. buttered cracker crumbs
1 tsp. chili powder (optional)

Cook spaghetti in boiling salted water for 8 minutes. Stir in oil. Drain. Sauté onion in butter until tender (green and red pepper can also be added for color). Blend in flour. Add broth gradually, stirring constantly until thickened. Add salts, milk, soup and cheese. Heat until cheese melts; combine with spaghetti. Put in baking dish and top with buttered cracker crumbs. Bake at 350° for 45 minutes. This recipe x4 fills a Lifetime roaster.

Chicken Rice Casserole

LUKE & KATHRYN MILLER

1 pt. chicken with broth
¾ c. mayonnaise
1 sm. onion
1 (10½) oz. can cream of
   chicken soup
1 c. diced celery
3½ c. cooked rice

Topping:
4 Tbsp. butter, melted
3½ c. Rice Krispies

Cook rice and add to the rest of the ingredients and place into a 9"x13" pan. *For Topping:* Mix together and sprinkle on top. Bake at 350° for 1 hour.

Chicken and Rice Casserole

LARRY & NAOMI LENGACHER

chicken pcs., your choice how
   many
1 c. onion
2 cans cream of mushroom soup
2 cans cream of chicken soup
4 c. water
1½ c. rice
8-10 slices Velveeta cheese
cornflakes, for on top (optional)
1 can chicken broth

Mix everything together. Put in medium roaster at 400°. Keep covered till rice is soft. A favorite of ours.

101

Meats & Main Dishes

Chicken Enchilada

ED & MARY SLABAUGH

½ c. chopped onion
4 Tbsp. butter
¼ c. flour
2 c. chicken broth
1 tsp. chicken base
8 oz. sour cream
3 c. cooked chicken
2-3 c. cheddar or mozzarella
cheese
1 tsp. chili powder
10-12 flour tortillas
1 can salsa sauce or
1 can enchilada sauce

Sauté onions in butter. Stir in flour, chicken broth and base. Cook until thickened. Remove from heat and add sour cream. In mixing bowl combine chicken, 1 c. of the chicken broth mixture, 1 c. cheese and chili powder. Place 2 Tbsp. meat mixture in each tortilla. Roll up and place in a 9"x13" pan lined with sauce. Put remaining chicken broth mixture over all and top with remaining cheese. Bake at 350° for 25 minutes. Serves 6 to 8.

Chicken Breast Casserole

MARY LENGACHER

102

4 boneless chicken breasts
4 slices cheese
½ c. sour cream
½ c. milk
1 can cream of mushroom or
cream of chicken soup
1 box chicken stuffing

Place chicken breasts in bottom of pan, casserole dish or small roaster. Place slice of cheese on each piece. Mix together sour cream, milk and soup. Pour over breasts. Melt 3 Tbsp. butter and toss with 2 c. chicken stuffing (1 box). Put on top, cover, and bake at 350° for 1½ hours.

Chicken on Sunday

STEVE & MIRIAM LENGACHER

2 c. uncooked rice
1 can cream of mushroom soup
1 can cream of celery soup
2 soup cans of water
½ c. milk
1 chicken, cut up
1 pkg. onion soup mix
seasoning to taste

Grease casserole or a 9"x13" pan. Sprinkle rice in bottom. Mix soups with water and milk; pour over rice. Lay chicken pieces on top. Sprinkle with onion soup mix and seasonings. Cover pan and bake at 325° for 2½ hours. Serves 8 to 10.

Ultimate Chicken Fingers

JAY & AMY TROYER

1 lb. (3) chicken breasts
⅔ c. Bisquick
½ c. Parmesan cheese
½ tsp. salt or garlic salt
½ tsp. paprika
1 egg, beaten
3 Tbsp. butter, melted

Cut chicken in ½" strips. Mix Bisquick, Parmesan and seasoning. Dip chicken in egg and coat with Bisquick mixture. Place on pan and drizzle with melted butter. Bake at 450° for approx. 12-14 minutes, turning halfway through baking time. Serves 4.

103

Pretzel-Coated Chicken

MATTHEW & MARLENE TROYER

32 chicken tenders, soaked in
   your favorite marinade
3 garlic cloves, minced
½ c. buttermilk
½ tsp. pepper
½ tsp. salt
3 eggs
¾ c. flour
6 c. pretzels, sourdough or Unique
⅔ c. mayonnaise
2 Tbsp. brown spicy mustard
1 tsp. sugar, rounded

Put pretzels in blender until finely crushed. Place pretzels and flour in separate bowls. In third bowl, beat eggs, buttermilk, garlic, pepper and salt. Dip chicken in flour, then egg mixture, then in pretzel crumbs. Fry in olive oil for 5 minutes on each side. Mix mayonnaise, mustard and sugar. Serve with chicken. Serves 12.

Parmesan Chicken

JACOB & LORETTA WEAVER

4 chicken breasts
1 c. crushed cracker crumbs
½ c. Parmesan cheese
½ tsp. chicken seasoning
1 tsp. seasoning salt
¼ tsp. black pepper
½ c. melted butter

Cut chicken in half lengthwise and "widthwise". Roll chicken in butter, then in crumb mixture. Drizzle leftover butter on top. Bake at 350° for 1 hour.

104

Honey-Baked Chicken

JOHN & ESTA YODER

⅓ c. melted butter
¼ c. honey
1 tsp. salt
2 Tbsp. prepared mustard

Heat. Pour over chicken and bake at 350° for 45 minutes. Turn chicken around and bake another 30-40 minutes. You need to double the sauce for a 9"x13" pan of chicken.

Sweet and Sour Chicken

IVAN & BARBARA SCHLABACH

10 lb. boneless chicken
Zesty Italian dressing
meat tenderizer

Sauce:
1 pt. water
1 pt. vinegar
1 Tbsp. salt
2 lb. brown sugar
⅓ c. Perma-Flo

Marinate chicken at least 3 days with Zesty Italian dressing and meat tenderizer. Grill and layer with sauce. Bake breasts at 175° and thighs at 200°. *Sauce:* Stir everything together and heat until thickened.

105

Ground Chicken Patties

MATTHIAS & NAOMI MAST

5 lb. ground chicken
1 Tbsp. salt
1 Tbsp. Lawry's seasoned salt
1 tsp. black pepper
1 bag crackers, crushed

Mix well, form into patties and dip in breading mix. Fry or grill.

Chicken Marinade

JUSTIN & NAOMI MILLER

3 c. water
¾ c. vinegar
¼ c. sugar
¾ c. butter
1 Tbsp. garlic salt
1 Tbsp. Worcestershire sauce
¼ c. salt
¼ c. corn syrup
1 Tbsp. black pepper

Mix all ingredients together. Cook until dissolved; pour over chicken. Will do 10 lb. chicken.

Marinade for Chicken

STEVIE & REBECCA SWAREY

2½ qt. water
1 c. salt
1 qt. vinegar
¾ c. Worcestershire sauce

Soak chicken pieces in brine for 24 hours. Grill.

106

Coating for Baked Chicken

STEVIE & REBECCA SWAREY

2 c. cracker & cornflake crumbs
½ c. cornmeal (optional)
3 tsp. seasoning salt
1 tsp. paprika
1 tsp. ground mustard
½ tsp. garlic powder
1½ tsp. pepper

Roll chicken in milk or butter. Roll in crumbs. Bake at 400° for 30 minutes, then at 350° for 1 hour or till done. Cornmeal gives it a good taste and crunch.

Chicken Coating

ENOS & NANCY TROYER

½ c. flour
2 tsp. paprika
1 tsp. black pepper
¼ tsp. dry mustard
3 tsp. salt

Melt butter on cookie sheet or cake pan; dip chicken pieces in milk, then in this flour mixture. Bake at 400° for 1 hour or more.

Curly Fry Casserole

MATTHIAS & NAOMI MAST

2 lb. hamburger, fried
1 can refried beans
1 pkg. taco seasoning
2 c. sour cream
2 cans cream of chicken soup
¾ c. taco sauce
1 pkg. tortilla shells
shredded cheese
curly fries

Fry hamburger and add beans and taco seasoning. Mix together sour cream, cream of chicken soup and taco sauce and add to first mixture. Cut up tortilla shells and add to meat mixture. Top with shredded cheese and curly fries. Bake until heated through.

107

Taco Bake

JOSEPH & RHODA MILLER

2 lb. hamburger, browned with
    onion, salt, pepper and Lawry's
1 pt. pizza sauce
1 c. ketchup
½ c. water
⅔ c. quick oats
¾ c. brown sugar
1 pkg. taco seasoning

Cream Mixture:
8 oz. cream cheese
16 oz. sour cream

Brown hamburger with onions, salt, pepper and Lawry's. Then add rest of ingredients. Put cream mixture on top of a 12"x17" pan of crescent rolls. Top with hamburger mixture, then put shredded cheddar cheese on top. Bake at 350° until center is hot. Serve with salsa, lettuce, sweet and sour dressing and Doritos (crushed). Serves 12.

Deep-Dish Taco Squares

SAMUEL & LEANNA WEAVER

108

2 lb. ground beef, browned with
    1 onion
¾ c. sour cream
⅔ c. Miracle Whip
1 c. shredded cheese
1 c. salsa
Biscuit dough (see page 25)

Put Biscuit dough in greased 9"x13" glass pan. Top with browned beef and onion. Mix sour cream and Miracle Whip; add cheese. Layer salsa on top of meat, then spoon sour cream mixture over top. Bake at 350° for 30-40 minutes. Serves 10.

Simple Taco Salad

JUSTIN & NAOMI MILLER

2 c. flour
2 tsp. sugar
½ tsp. salt
⅔ c. milk
4 tsp. baking powder
½ tsp. cream of tartar
½ c. shortening
1½ lb. hamburger
1 pkg. taco seasoning
1 pt. pizza sauce
16 oz. sour cream
8 oz. cream cheese
lettuce
tomatoes
grated cheese
taco chips, crushed
hot sauce

Combine first 7 ingredients and spread in an 11"x17" cookie sheet with sides. Bake at 350°. Mix sour cream and cream cheese and spread on cooled crust. Brown hamburger and season with taco seasoning and pizza sauce. When cooled, spread on top of sour cream layer. Top with shredded cheese. Serve with lettuce, tomatoes, taco chips and hot sauce. Cut into squares before putting lettuce and tomatoes on top.

109

Burrito Casserole

JOSIAH & SUSAN MILLER

18 lb. hamburger
3 (15 oz.) cans refried beans
3 (26 oz.) cans cream of
   mushroom soup
3 (26 oz.) cans cream of chicken
   soup
6 pt. sour cream
4 qt. taco sauce or pizza sauce
3-4 pkg. tortillas
shredded cheddar cheese
3 pkg. taco seasoning

Fry hamburger with onions, taco seasoning, salt and pepper. Add beans and rest of ingredients, except for tortillas and cheese. Layer in roasters, hamburger and tortillas, cut in bite size pieces. Repeat layers and end with hamburger. After heated through put shredded cheese on top and melt. Makes an electric roaster full plus a round Lifetime. Serves 100.

Meats & Main Dishes

Chimichangas

JAY & AMY TROYER

3 lb. hamburger with onion
2 pkg. taco seasoning
½ tsp. garlic salt
1 tsp. cumin
1 c. shredded cheese
2 pkg. tortillas

OR

2 c. diced chicken
2 c. shredded mozzarella cheese
2 tsp. parsley
½ tsp. garlic salt
½ tsp. salt
¼ tsp. pepper
6-8 tortillas

Mix either hamburger or chicken mixture. Warm tortillas and put ½ c. mixture on each tortilla. Fold up to make a square and insert toothpicks to secure. Deep-fry, bottom first, at 375°. Serve with lettuce, tomato, sour cream and peppers. Top with cheese sauce.

110

Hamburger Cheese Bake

MATTHEW & MARLENE TROYER

1½-2 lb. hamburger
1½ c. uncooked rice
2⅔ c. water
1 c. shredded mozzarella cheese
1½ c. cubed Velveeta cheese
2 cans cream of mushroom soup
1⅓ c. milk

Cook meat until done. Place rice in a greased 9"x13" pan. Place meat and Velveeta cubes over rice. Mix soup, water and milk, pour over top. Sprinkle with mozzarella, cover and bake at 350° for 1½ hours or until rice is done. Serves 6 to 8.

Spaghetti Pie

VERNON & RUTH YODER

18 lb. hamburger, fried
11 qt. spaghetti or pizza sauce
5 lb. rotini
12 lb. sour cream
16 oz. cream cheese
2-3 lb. shredded mozzarella cheese
salt & pepper to taste
chopped onion
Parmesan cheese

Brown hamburger; add salt, pepper and onions. Stir sauce into meat. Cook rotini and gently stir into meat mixture. Place in baking dish. Combine sour cream and cream cheese; spread over rotini and sprinkle with shredded cheese. Top with Parmesan cheese. Bake at 350°, covered. Serves 130.

Spaghetti Casserole

JOSIAH & RHODA MILLER

16 oz. pkg. angel-hair pasta
1½ lb. hamburger
1 qt. pizza sauce
2 (8 oz.) cans tomato sauce or
    thick tomato juice
1 can mushroom soup
1 c. sour cream
2 c. shredded cheese

Cook pasta according to directions. Drain pasta. Brown hamburger and add pizza sauce and tomato sauce. Mix together mushroom soup and sour cream. Grease 9"x13" pan and put half of meat mixture in pan, then half of pasta and half of soup mixture. Repeat layers. Top with cheese. Bake at 350° for 1 hour.

111

Zucchini Casserole

VERNON & RUTH YODER

2 lb. hamburger
4 c. zucchini, grated
1 c. mushroom soup
1½-2 c. milk
salt
pepper
Lawry's salt
toasted bread crumbs
Velveeta cheese

Brown hamburger. Cook zucchini in a little water until soft. Mix everything together except bread crumbs and Velveeta and bake in a 9"x13" pan at 350° for about 15 minutes. Add cheese and bread crumbs and put in oven till cheese is melted. Serves 10.

Zucchini Pancakes

MATTHEW & MARLENE TROYER

⅔ c. Bisquick
¼ c. Parmesan cheese
2 eggs
2 c. shredded zucchini
⅛ tsp. black pepper
⅛ tsp. salt

Combine all ingredients except zucchini. When ready to fry, add zucchini. Mix well and drop ¼ c. onto skillet. Use butter or olive oil to fry till golden brown. These are delicious served with a little maple syrup. Serves 3 to 4.

Zucchini Bake

MATTHEW & MARLENE TROYER

1 c. Bisquick
½ c. shredded cheese
2 Tbsp. parsley
¾ tsp. seasoned salt
½ tsp. marjoram
½ c. olive oil
3 c. shredded zucchini
¼ c. chopped onion
1 clove garlic, minced
3 eggs, beaten

Mix dry ingredients, then add everything except zucchini. Fold in zucchini and spread in a 9"x13" pan. Bake at 350° till light brown, about 25-30 minutes. Serves 8.

Zucchini Lasagna

LUKE & KATHRYN MILLER

1 lb. ground beef
¼ c. chopped onion
1 c. (15 oz.) tomato sauce
½ tsp. salt
½ tsp. oregano
½ tsp. basil
¼ tsp. black pepper
4 med. zucchini (1¼ lb.)
1 c. cottage cheese
1 egg, beaten
3 Tbsp. flour
1 c. shredded mozzarella cheese

Brown beef and onion. Add tomato sauce and seasonings. Bring to boil, simmer 5 minutes. Slice zucchini lengthwise into ¼" slices. In a small bowl, combine cottage cheese and egg. In a 9"x13" pan, place half the zucchini and sprinkle with half the flour. Top with cheese mixture and half the meat. Repeat layer of zucchini and flour. Sprinkle with mozzarella cheese and remaining meat. Bake at 375° for 40 minutes or until heated through. Remove from oven and sprinkle with additional cheese.

113

Meats & Main Dishes

Zucchini Lasagna

MATTHEW & MARLENE TROYER

zucchini
flour
salt
pepper
eggs, beaten
spaghetti sauce
mushrooms
Parmesan cheese
mozzarella cheese

Slice zucchini; roll in eggs, then in flour. Fry and drain on paper towel. Put spaghetti sauce in bottom of a baking dish, the size you need. Layer in order, zucchini, sauce, mushrooms, Parmesan cheese and mozzarella cheese. Put on as many layers as desired. When frying zucchini sprinkle with salt and pepper. Bake at 350° till bubbly and hot.

Veggie Meatball Casserole

MATTHIAS & NAOMI MAST

1 lb. potatoes
1 lb. carrots
1 lb. meatballs
½ c. butter
½ c. flour
1 qt. water
1 pkg. onion soup mix
2 Tbsp. Worcestershire sauce
1 Tbsp. garlic salt
½ c. Velveeta cheese
1½ c. sour cream

Cube potatoes and carrots. Cook until tender. Form meatballs and bake until golden brown and no longer pink in the middle. Melt butter, blend in flour slowly. Add water, heat until thickened. Add seasonings, cheese and sour cream. Pour over prepared veggies and meatballs. Heat. Bake 2 tubes biscuits, cut into 8 pieces and put on top when ready to serve.

114

Ham Loaf

MATTHIAS & NAOMI MAST

2 lb. ground smoked ham
1 lb. ground fresh ham
1 c. crushed crackers
1 c. milk
2 eggs

Glaze:
1 c. brown sugar
⅓ c. vinegar

Simmer glaze while mixing ham. Mix ham ingredients well and form loaves or balls. Pour glaze over ham and bake at 325° for 1½–2 hours. Baste every 15 minutes.

½-¾ c. water

Meatloaf

STEVE & MIRIAM LENGACHER

1 egg, beaten
¼ c. onion
2 tsp. salt
⅛ tsp. chili powder
¼ tsp. pepper
1 c. quick oats
1 Tbsp. ketchup
1 c. milk
1½ lb. hamburger

Sauce:
⅓ c. ketchup
¼ tsp. mustard
2 Tbsp. brown sugar

115

Meatballs

VERNON & RUTH YODER

3 lb. ground beef
1 (12 oz.) can evaporated milk
1 c. oatmeal
1 c. cracker crumbs
2 eggs
½ c. chopped onions
½ tsp. garlic powder
2 tsp. salt
½ tsp. pepper
2 tsp. chili powder

Combine milk, oatmeal, cracker crumbs, eggs, onions, garlic powder, salt, pepper and chili powder. Add ground beef and mix well. Form into balls and bake in cookie sheet with sides at 350° for about ½ hour or until done. Place meatballs in casserole and pour sauce over meatballs. Return to oven and heat through.

Sauce:
2 c. ketchup
1 c. brown sugar
½ tsp. Liquid Smoke or suit to taste
½ tsp. garlic powder, scant
¼ c. chopped onions

Honey Barbecue Meatballs

MELISSA ANN SCHLABACH

3 lb. hamburger
1 c. crushed crackers
1 c. oatmeal
1 can evaporated milk
2 eggs
2 tsp. salt
1 tsp. chili powder
½ tsp. garlic salt
½ tsp. pepper
onion to taste

Bake on cookie sheet for ½ hour. Put in roaster and layer with barbecue sauce.

Honey Barbecue Sauce:
2 c. ketchup
¾ c. honey
1 c. brown sugar
½ tsp. garlic salt
½ tsp. pepper
1 tsp. liquid smoke
1 Tbsp. spicy brown mustard
1 Tbsp. Worcestershire sauce

Tangy Meatballs

JOSIAH & RHODA MILLER

2 eggs
2 c. oatmeal
1 c. evaporated milk
1 c. chopped onion
2 tsp. salt
½ tsp. pepper
½ tsp. garlic powder
3 lb. ground beef

Sauce:
2 c. ketchup
1 c. brown sugar
½ c. chopped onion

Mix and shape into small balls. Bake at 375° for 20 minutes, then layer with sauce and return to oven and bake 30 minutes longer. I use my small cookie dropper (making it rounded) to shape the balls. 1 batch makes around 90 meatballs.

1½ tsp. Liquid Smoke
½ tsp. garlic powder

Barbecued Meatballs

JACOB & LORETTA WEAVER

3 lb. ground beef or venison
2 c. quick oats
1½ c. milk (can use evaporated)
2 eggs, beaten
½ c. chopped onions
2 tsp. chili powder
3 tsp. salt
½ tsp. garlic powder
½ tsp. pepper

Sauce:
4 c. ketchup
1½ c. brown sugar
½ c. chopped onions (optional)
3 Tbsp. Liquid Smoke
1 tsp. garlic powder

117

Mix meatball ingredients well. Shape into small balls. Place single layer in baking pans. Combine sauce ingredients and pour over meatballs. Bake at 350° until done, approx. 45 minutes. Or freeze in portions for later use. *To Freeze Meatballs:* Place raw meatballs single layer on cookie sheets, freeze until solid. Store frozen balls in freezer bag until ready to use. Very handy! We enjoy these tasty meatballs often.

Meats & Main Dishes

Tangy Meatballs

LUKE & KATHRYN MILLER

2 eggs
2 c. quick oats
1 can evaporated milk
1 c. chopped onion
2 tsp. salt
½ tsp. pepper
½ tsp. garlic powder
3 lb. ground beef

Sauce:
2 c. ketchup
1 c. brown sugar
½ c. chopped onion
1½ tsp. Liquid Smoke
½ tsp. garlic powder

In large bowl, beat eggs. Add onions, milk, oats, salt, pepper, garlic powder and ground beef. Mix well. Shape into balls. Bake uncovered on cookie sheet at 375° for 30 minutes. Remove from oven and drain. Place all meatballs in roaster. In saucepan bring all sauce ingredients to a boil. Pour over meatballs. Return to oven and bake uncovered for 20 minutes or until meatballs are done.

Our Favorite Sauerkraut

MATTHEW & MARLENE TROYER

2 qt. rinsed & drained kraut
1¼ c. applesauce
½-¾ c. maple syrup or
   brown sugar

Layer in baking dish with sausage or kielbasa. Bake at 375° for 1 hour. Delicious on mashed potatoes. Serves 6 to 8.

Sauerkraut

MATTHIAS & NAOMI MAST

2 bags sauerkraut, rinsed & drained
1 c. water
½ c. butter or coconut oil
¼ c. brown sugar or maple syrup

Mix all together in baking dish or crockpot and bake at 300° for 3-4 hours. If adding fully cooked meat, add last hour of baking time.

Farmhouse Kitchen

MARY LENGACHER

1
1
1 eg
mill
pinch of parsley with flour
   (optional)

Mix flour and baking powder; add beaten egg and some milk, just to moisten. Drop by spoonfuls into hot broth, cover, and boil till dumplings are big and light, approx. 10 minutes. Beef broth may be used too.

A simple and quick meal for children.

Campfire Stew

LEAH TROYER

1½ c. butter
1 lg. onion, chopped
2 lb. hamburger
3 qt. chicken broth
3 qt. beef broth
3 lb. carrots, cut up
4 qt. potatoes, cut up
4 lb. sausage links
1¾ c. flour
⅔ c. cornstarch
2 Tbsp. brown sugar
1 tsp. garlic salt
2 tsp. onion salt
2 tsp. salt
1 tsp. pepper
2 tsp. Lawry's salt
3 tsp. Nature's salt
3 Tbsp. beef base

In large iron kettle, brown onions in butter, then fry hamburger. Add broth and bring to boil. Add carrots and wait for 10 minutes, then add potatoes and seasonings. When veggies are almost tender add flour, cornstarch and sugar that has been mixed together. Stir constantly. When thickened, add sausage.

119

Meats & Main Dishes

Baked Beans

VERNON & RUTH YODER

1 can dark red kidney beans
1 can sm. lima beans
1 med. can pork & beans
½ lb. bacon, cut in strips
2 sm. onions, chopped
¾ c. brown sugar
1 c. ketchup
1 tsp. prepared mustard

Mix beans together including juice. Cook bacon in skillet, but don't brown completely. Add onions, sugar, ketchup and mustard. Heat through and pour over beans and mix well. Bake at 350° in open casserole for 1 hour or more.

Calico Baked Beans

ATLEE & MATTIE MILLER

32 oz. pork & beans
16 oz. kidney beans
16 oz. sm. butter beans
2 lb. bacon, fried
1 chopped, onion
¼ c. bacon drippings
1 c. ketchup
1 c. brown sugar
1 Tbsp. mustard
1 Tbsp. vinegar

Drain beans. Sauté onions in ¼ c. bacon drippings and mix together ketchup, brown sugar, mustard and vinegar. Add sauce and bacon drippings and onions to beans. Bake at 350° for 1 hour. May top with sour cream and crushed corn chips just before serving.

For special flavor add 1 can pineapple tidbits.

120

Corn Fritters

ED & MARY SLABAUGH

2 c. creamed corn
2 eggs
¼ c. flour
1 tsp. salt
⅛ tsp. pepper
1 tsp. baking powder
2 Tbsp. milk

Mix and drop by tablespoon in frying pan in 4 Tbsp. oil. Serves 4.

Cornbread Casserole

JOSIAH & SUSAN MILLER

1 pt. whole corn
1 pt. creamed corn
1 c. cornmeal
1 egg
2 Tbsp. butter, melted
1 Tbsp. vegetable oil
3 Tbsp. sour cream
1 tsp. soda
1½ tsp. salt
¼ tsp. garlic powder
¼ tsp. paprika

In a large bowl, combine all ingredients. Pour into greased 11"x7"x2" baking dish. Bake uncovered at 400° for 25-30 minutes or until top edges are golden brown.

121

Grandma's Gravy

JOSIAH & RHODA MILLER

1 c. Crisco
1½ c. flour
water
1 can evaporated milk
2-3 tsp. salt
pepper to taste

Brown Crisco and flour in large skillet, stirring all the while. Brown well. Add water till skillet is about full. Bring to boiling. Remove from heat and add milk, salt and pepper.

Cheese Sauce

MICHAEL & JOANNE COBLENTZ

2 Tbsp. flour
2 Tbsp. butter
½ tsp. salt
1 c. milk
½ c. Velveeta cheese

In a 1 qt. pan melt butter, flour and salt. Slowly add milk. When thickened, add cheese. Very simple and delicious!

Crumbs for Deep-Fried Fish

STEVIE & REBECCA SWAREY

1 pkg. crackers, crushed
2 tsp. Old Bay or
   Cape Cod seasoning
1 tsp. Season-All salt
¼ tsp. garlic powder
2 tsp. lemon pepper
⅛ tsp. dill weed
⅛ tsp. pepper
½ tsp. salt
2 eggs, beaten

Beat eggs; dip fish in eggs, then in crumbs. Deep-fat-fry. Delicious!

Marinade for Steak and Pork Chops

STEVIE & REBECCA SWAREY

½ c. butter
⅓ c. lemon juice
⅓ c. ketchup
4-5 Tbsp. Worcestershire sauce
2 Tbsp. apple cider vinegar
2 Tbsp. vegetable oil
2 tsp. garlic powder
1 tsp. sugar
1 tsp. salt
dash of hot pepper sauce

Melt butter; add rest of ingredients. Soak meat overnight or for 24 hours. Grill. Sprinkle steak with seasonings, let set 5 minutes, flip and repeat other side. Grill.

Steak Seasoning:
2 tsp. garlic powder
2 tsp. onion powder
½ tsp. black pepper
2 tsp. Seasona-All
2 tsp. paprika

123

Oven Barbecued Pork Ribs

STEVIE & REBECCA SWAREY

1½ c. water
1 c. ketchup
⅓ c. Worcestershire sauce
1 tsp. salt
1 tsp. chili powder
½ tsp. onion powder
⅛ tsp. hot pepper sauce
3-4 lb. pork ribs

Place ribs in a roasting pan. Bake uncovered at 350° for 45 minutes. Meanwhile, in a saucepan, combine rest of ingredients. Bring to a boil, cook for 1 minute. Drain ribs and spoon sauce over ribs. Cover and bake 1½ hours, uncover and bake 30 minutes more, basting once. Total baking time: 2 hours and 45 minutes.

RECIPE FOR _____

_____
_____
_____
_____
_____
_____
_____
_____
_____
_____
_____
_____
_____

RECIPE FOR _____

_____
_____
_____
_____
_____
_____
_____
_____
_____
_____
_____
_____
_____

Pizzas and Sandwiches

Taco Pizza

MATTHEW & MARLENE TROYER

pizza crust
1½ lb. fried hamburger
2 Tbsp. taco seasoning
⅔ c. mayonnaise
16 oz. sour cream
¼ c. sugar
shredded cheese
nacho tortilla chips

Bake crust until almost done. Mix taco seasoning and hamburger and put on top of crust. Combine mayonnaise, sour cream and sugar. Spread on top of hamburger. Bake until done. Put cheese and chips on top and bake until cheese is melted. Add tomatoes if desired.

BLT Pizza

MATTHIAS & NAOMI MAST

1 prepared pizza crust

Spread pizza sauce and cheese onto crust. Bake to desired doneness. Spread with a little veggie dip or sour cream. Top with bacon, lettuce and tomato. Serve immediately.

Potato Pizza Bake

MATTHIAS & NAOMI MAST

7 c. potatoes
onion
1 can cream of soup
  of your choice
salt, pepper & garlic salt to taste

Shred potatoes; add chopped onion, soup and spices. Put in 11"x17" cookie sheet and bake at 350° for 45 minutes-1 hour, until soft. Top with 1 c. sour cream, 1 lb. fried hamburger, mushrooms, pepperoni and mozzarella cheese. Bake another 10 minutes.

Bubble Pizza

MARY LENGACHER

2 (12 oz.) cans buttermilk
   biscuits
1½ lb. sausage, browned
1 c. pizza sauce or more
1 can cream of mushroom soup
cheese

Cut each biscuit into 8 pieces and toss into a greased 9"x13" pan. Mix together browned sausage, pizza sauce and mushroom soup. Pour over biscuits. Add whatever toppings you prefer—peppers, onions, pepperoni, etc. Bake at 350° for about 20 minutes. Top with cheese and bake until done.

Note: I use 1 pt. pizza sauce.

Good Pizza

SAMUEL & LEANNA WEAVER

1 c. hot water
2 Tbsp. butter
2 Tbsp. sugar
1 Tbsp. instant yeast
½ tsp. basil (dried)
¼ tsp. garlic powder
½ tsp. salt
½ tsp. oregano
2½-3 c. Prairie Gold flour
   Toppings:
1 pt. pizza sauce
¼ c. chopped onion
¼ c. chopped pepper
¼ c. mushrooms
2 lb. sausage or ground beef
2 c. shredded cheese

Mix first 3 ingredients. Let set till butter is soft and water is cool enough, then add next 6 ingredients. Press into large (half sheet) greased cookie sheet. Spread 1 pt. pizza sauce on crust and top with peppers, onions, mushrooms, and your choice of meat. Bake at 375° for 20 minutes. Top with cheese. Return to oven for 3 minutes or till cheese is melted. Serves 10.

127

Delicious Barbecue Pizza

CHARITY SCHLABACH

2 Tbsp. yeast
2/3 c. warm water
2 tsp. sugar
2 c. cold water
3 Tbsp. vegetable oil
2 Tbsp. sugar
1/4 tsp. garlic salt
1/4 tsp. oregano
6-6 1/2 c. flour

Toppings:
pineapple
barbecue sauce
chicken (cooked in Italian)
onions
banana peppers
bacon
cheese
basil (optional)

Combine first 3 ingredients. Let set 5 minutes. Add remaining ingredients, adding only 1/2 c. of the flour. Mix well. Add flour till workable. Let rise till doubled. Oil two large pans well. Sprinkle with cornmeal. Press dough into pans. Let rise for 1/2 hour. Bake at 400° about 7 minutes. Top with pineapple sauce, chicken, onions, peppers and bacon. Bake at 350° till heated. Add cheese. Bake till melted. Sprinkle with basil and serve.

128

Buffalo Chicken Pizza

JAY & AMY TROYER

1 pizza crust
2 c. grilled or cooked chicken
1/3 c. hot sauce
2 Tbsp. butter, melted
1 c. pizza sauce
2 c. shredded cheese
1/2 c. ranch dressing

Combine chicken (chopped), hot sauce and butter, set aside. Spread pizza sauce over crust and top with chicken mixture. Top with cheese. Bake 15-18 minutes. Top with ranch dressing.

Chicken Pizza Barbecue Sauce

ATLEE & MATTIE MILLER

1 c. ketchup
½ c. brown sugar
⅓ c. white sugar
¼ c. honey
2 tsp. mustard
1½ tsp. Worcestershire sauce
¼ tsp. salt
¼ tsp. Liquid Smoke
¼ tsp. black pepper
1 Tbsp. lemon juice

Blend together and heat to a boil. Put in pt. jar and keep in refrigerator. Good and handy for dipping or burgers.

Sub Sandwich Bread

JUSTIN & NAOMI MILLER

129

2 c. hot water
2 Tbsp. sugar
2 Tbsp. margarine
2 tsp. salt
2 Tbsp. yeast
1 Tbsp. sugar
½ c. warm water
6 c. all-purpose flour, divided

Mix hot water, sugar, margarine and salt; cool down, then add yeast, sugar and warm water. Mix thoroughly. Add 2½ c. flour; whip until smooth. Add rest of flour. Let rise until double, then punch down every 10 minutes 3 times. Divide dough in 4 parts. Spread out ½" thick, 5" wide. Roll up like rolls and flatten out a bit. Let rise until double, then put on greased cookie sheets. Beat 1 egg; mix in 1 Tbsp. milk. Brush on top of sub bread. Make cuts ¼" deep, 1" apart across top of bread. Bake at 400° for 10 minutes. Cut through middle and fix with meats and cheese. Put back in oven till cheese is melted. Top with peppers, onions and tomatoes or fix to personal preference. Enjoy!

Chicken Sandwiches

MARCUS & ROSANNA MAST

2 c. milk
2 tsp. salt
5 Tbsp. flour
¼ c. butter
¼ tsp. pepper
2 eggs, beaten
4 c. diced chicken
Velveeta cheese
onions

Make white sauce of milk, flour, butter and seasonings. Add eggs, cheese and onions. Pour over chicken and stir. Serve hot.

Chicken Sandwiches

MARY LENGACHER

3 c. chicken meat, cut fine
1½ c. cracker crumbs
2 c. chicken broth or part water
chicken base to taste
salt & pepper to taste

Mix all ingredients together. Bake at 325°. Stir once in a while, so it will not get brown or too dry. Cover and keep hot till ready to use. Put on buns and serve.

Big Mac Sandwiches

MATTHIAS & NAOMI MAST

buns
thin prepared hamburgers
hash browns
Big Mac sauce
lettuce

Spread Big Mac sauce onto buns and top with hamburgers, hash browns and lettuce.

130

Big Mac Sandwiches

JAY & AMY TROYER

Sauce:
1 c. Miracle Whip
⅓ c. pickle relish
¼ c. French dressing
1 Tbsp. minced onion
1 Tbsp. sugar
1 tsp. pepper

Combine sauce ingredients; spread on buns.

Put on each sandwich:

sauce
onions
hash browns

hamburgers
pickles
lettuce

Big Mac Sauce

MATTHIAS & NAOMI MAST

1 c. Miracle Whip
⅓ c. pepper or pickle relish
¼ c. French dressing
1 Tbsp. minced onion
1 Tbsp. sugar
¼ tsp. black pepper

Mix together and serve on barbecued hamburgers or other sandwiches. Made 10 batches for 120 sandwiches.

131

Pizza Crust

JUSTIN & NAOMI MILLER

⅔ c. warm water
¼ c. vegetable oil
¾ Tbsp. sugar
¼ tsp. salt
½ Tbsp. yeast
1½ c. flour

Let rise 20-30 minutes, then put in 12" round pizza pan. Let rise. Bake at 375° for 8-10 minutes. Add toppings and bake 12-15 minutes longer.

Pizza Crust

MICHAEL & JOANNE COBLENTZ

1 c. warm water
1 Tbsp. sugar
⅜ c. vegetable oil
¼ tsp. salt
oregano
¾ Tbsp. yeast
2¼ c. flour

Mix together and let rise for 20-30 minutes. Press into greased 11"x17" pan and let rise. Bake at 375° for 8 minutes. Top with sauce and pizza toppings and return to oven for another 12-15 minutes.

132

Pizza Crust

JAY & AMY TROYER

2 Tbsp. yeast
2⅔ c. warm water
2 Tbsp. + 2 tsp. sugar
3 Tbsp. vegetable oil
¼ tsp. garlic salt
¼ tsp. Italian seasoning
½ tsp. oregano
6-6½ c. flour

Mix ingredients with ½ of flour until smooth. Add remaining flour. Let rise. Grease pans and press dough into pans. Bake at 400° for 8-10 minutes. Top with any of your favorite toppings. Yield: 2 large crusts.

Pizza Dough

JACOB & LORETTA WEAVER

1 c. warm water
1-2 Tbsp. sugar
1 Tbsp. yeast
¼ c. vegetable oil
dash salt
2½ c. flour

Put warm water, yeast and sugar in bowl and mix. Add vegetable oil, salt and flour; mix well. Sometimes I add Italian seasoning and garlic powder, etc. in the dough also. Grease pan lightly with oil. Press dough into 11"x17" pan. Let rise slightly; prebake. Add sauce and toppings of your choice. Enjoy!

Pizza Crust

MATTHIAS & NAOMI MAST

1 c. water
1 Tbsp. yeast (reg. or instant)
1 Tbsp. brown sugar
2 Tbsp. vegetable oil
1 Tbsp. Miracle Whip
1 tsp. salt
2½ c. flour

This is just right for 2 (11"x17") pans.

133

Pizzas & Sandwiches

Vegetable Pizza

JACOB & LORETTA WEAVER

Crust:
3 c. flour
1½ Tbsp. sugar
4½ tsp. baking powder
1½ tsp. salt
1¼ c. milk
¾ c. butter, melted

Filling:
8 oz. cream cheese
1 pt. sour cream
1 pkg. or 3 Tbsp. ranch
 dressing mix

Topping:
chopped vegetables
bacon crumbles & shredded cheese

Mix ingredients for crust in order given. Press into 11"x17" pan and bake at 350° until done and should look soft, approx. 15 minutes. Do not allow to brown! Cool. Mix filling ingredients and spread on crust. Cut into desired size pieces before topping with chopped broccoli, cauliflower, carrots, etc, add bacon crumbles an shredded cheese. Chill and serve. Delicious!

Taco Pizza Bake

134

MATTHIAS & NAOMI MAST

Make vegetable pizza crust (following recipe) and bake. Top with pizza sauce, hamburger mixed with taco seasoning and cheese. Bake at 350° for 15 minutes. Serve with lettuce, tomato, pepper rings and ranch and sweet and sour dressing. I like to add 1 Tbsp. taco seasoning to sweet and sour dressing.

Vegetable Pizza

MATTHIAS & NAOMI MAST

¼ c. butter
2 Tbsp. cane sugar
¼ c. boiling water
1 Tbsp. yeast
¼ c. warm water
1 egg, beaten
1½ c. flour
1 tsp. salt

Topping:
8 oz. cream cheese
1 pkg. ranch dip mix
8 oz. sour cream
1 Tbsp. cane sugar

Cream butter and sugar; add boiling water; stir until butter is melted. Dissolve yeast in warm water. Add yeast and beaten egg to butter mixture. Add flour and salt and mix well. Spread into greased 11"x17" pan. Bake at 325° until golden. Mix topping ingredients and spread on cooled crust. Top with your favorite vegetables and cheese.

Chicken and Bacon Pizza Bake

MATTHIAS & NAOMI MAST

Make vegetable pizza crust (preceding recipe) and bake; top with ranch dressing. Add fried chicken pieces, bacon and cheese. Bake at 350° for 15 minutes. Serve with lettuce, tomatoes, peppers and ranch and sweet and sour dressing.

Barbecued Hamburgers

MATTHIAS & NAOMI MAST

1 lb. ground beef
½ c. milk
1 tsp. salt
½ c. cracker crumbs
1 sm. onion
¼ tsp. pepper

Mix together and grill or bake with barbecue sauce.

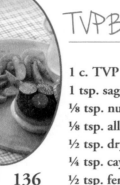

TVP Burgers

MATTHIAS & NAOMI MAST

1 c. TVP
1 tsp. sage
⅛ tsp. nutmeg
⅛ tsp. allspice
½ tsp. dry mustard
¼ tsp. cayenne
½ tsp. fennel
½ tsp. garlic powder
1 tsp. oregano
½ tsp. salt
¼ c. whole wheat flour

Combine all ingredients. Add 1 c. boiling water. Stir well. Let set 5 minutes. Add well beaten egg; form into patties and fry in a little butter and a little oil until browned on both sides.

136

Best-Ever Hamburgers

VERNON & RUTH YODER

1½ lb. ground beef
1 egg
⅓ c. quick oats
¼ tsp. onion salt
¼ tsp. garlic salt
¼ tsp. pepper
⅛ tsp. salt
1 c. cracker crumbs
½ c. milk

Mix together egg, crackers, oats, milk, salt, pepper, garlic salt and onion salt. Add ground beef and mix well. Shape into patties. Yield: approx. 12 patties.

Best Barbecue Burgers

JOSEPH & RHODA MILLER

1½ lb. hamburger
1 egg
⅓ c. oatmeal
¼ tsp. onion salt
¼ tsp. garlic salt
¼ tsp. pepper
⅛ tsp. salt
¼ c. sauce

Beat egg and add rest of ingredients and form into burgers. Grill, layering with sauce. Delicious and moist. Serves 8.

137

Sauce:
1 c. ketchup
½ c. brown sugar
¼ c. honey
2 tsp. mustard

1½ tsp. Worcestershire sauce
¼ tsp. salt
¼ tsp. Liquid Smoke
⅛ tsp. pepper

Pizzas & Sandwiches

RECIPE FOR _____

_____
_____
_____
_____
_____
_____
_____
_____
_____
_____
_____
_____
_____

RECIPE FOR _____

_____
_____
_____
_____
_____
_____
_____
_____
_____
_____
_____
_____
_____

Pies

Pie Crusts

MATTHIAS & NAOMI MAST

2 c. flour (Softex or Flaky Crust)
1 tsp. salt
1 tsp. baking powder
⅔ c. butter

Mix together until crumbly. In a small bowl mix 1 tsp. lecithin, 1½ tsp. vinegar and ⅓ c. cold water. Let set for a few minutes, then mix in with crumbs. Yield: 2-3 crusts.

Pie Crust Mix

JAMES & IDA LEHMAN

5 lb. flour
1 Tbsp. salt
1 Tbsp. baking powder
½ c. sugar
3 lb. butter flavored Crisco

In 7 qt. mixing bowl, mix first 4 ingredients. Cut in Crisco with pastry cutter until crumbly. Store in refrigerator until ready to use. Measure 1 c. mix to 2 Tbsp. water for 1 single crust pie.

Pie Crust

MARY LENGACHER

5⅓ c. flour
2 tsp. salt
2 c. butter Crisco
1 c. water or more

Mix flour, salt and Crisco together to fine crumbs. Add water till it forms a dough. If using pastry flour, use a little less Crisco. Yield 6-7 crusts. Freezes well.

Mom's Pumpkin Pie

MATTHIAS & NAOMI MAST

4 eggs, reserve 1 egg white &
   beat with 1 tsp. white sugar
1 c. brown sugar
½ c. sugar
2 Tbsp. flour
1½ c. pumpkin
2 tsp. vanilla
2 tsp. pumpkin pie spice
1 tsp. cinnamon
1 tsp. salt
4 c. rich milk

Beat eggs (saving 1 white). Add sugars and beat well; add flour, spices and pumpkin, beating after each addition. Scald milk and add. Beat egg white until stiff peaks form; add sugar. Mix with pumpkin mixture. Pour into 2 pie shells. Bake at 425° for 15 minutes, then at 350° for ½ hour.

Pumpkin Pie

LARRY & NAOMI LENGACHER

1½ c. pumpkin
3 Tbsp. flour, heaping
2 c. sugar (½ brown sugar)
4 c. milk, heated
1½ tsp. pumpkin pie spice
1½ tsp. cinnamon
1 tsp. salt
6 eggs, separated
3 tsp. vanilla
1 can Pet milk

Heat milk to scalding. In another bowl mix flour, sugar and spices, then add pumpkin and beaten egg yolks. Add milk. Last of all, add egg whites that have been beaten stiff. Bake at 400° for 10 minutes, then at 325° until done. Yield: 3 pies.

141

Pies

Pumpkin Pie

JAMES & IDA LEHMAN

1 c. pumpkin
1 c. sugar
1 c. brown sugar
3 Tbsp. flour
3 eggs, separated
1 tsp. salt
½ tsp. nutmeg
½ tsp. cinnamon
3 c. milk

Mix flour, sugar, spices and salt. Add egg yolks, pumpkin and milk. Beat egg whites till stiff and fold in last. Bake at 325° until firm. Serves 6.

Pumpkin Custard Pie

JACOB & LORETTA WEAVER

1 c. sugar
1 c. brown sugar
3 Tbsp. flour
½ tsp. salt
½ tsp. nutmeg
½ tsp. cinnamon
½ tsp. cloves
3 eggs, separated
1 c. pumpkin or squash
3 c. cold milk
2 unbaked pie crusts

Mix dry ingredients. Beat egg yolks, add milk and pumpkin. Beat all together. Beat egg whites until stiff. Fold into pumpkin mixture and beat again. It is important to keep it well beaten just before filling pies. Fills 2 pie crusts. Bake at 375° for 15 minutes; reduce heat to 300°. Bake until set.

142

Rhubarb Pie

MATTHIAS & NAOMI MAST

1 egg
1 c. cane sugar
1 tsp. vanilla
3 c. rhubarb
2 Tbsp. flour
3 Tbsp. cream or rich milk

Beat egg. Stir remaining ingredients with rhubarb, then add egg. Pour into pie crust and top with favorite crumbs. Bake at 400°-450° for 10-15 minutes, then at 350° for 30-40 minutes.

Sour Cream – Cream Cheese Pies

JAY & AMY TROYER

2 crusts
8 oz. cream cheese
1 c. sour cream
1 c. sugar
2 Tbsp. flour

Put cream cheese mixture into pie crusts, top with favorite pie filling. Put crust on top, brush with beaten egg whites, poke holes in crust and top with crumbs.

Crumbs:
½ c. flour
¼ c. brown sugar

⅛ c. butter

143

Pecan Pie

MARY LENGACHER

3 eggs
1 c. Karo
½ c. evaporated milk
½ c. brown sugar
1 Tbsp. flour
2 Tbsp. melted butter
1 tsp. vanilla
⅛ tsp. salt
1-1½ c. chopped pecans

Beat eggs; add all ingredients except pecans; mix well. Put pecans in bottom of 9" unbaked pie crust. Pour egg mixture in. Bake at 300° for 45 minutes or until done.

Pies

Vanilla Crumb Pie

MICHAEL & JOANNE COBLENTZ

8 oz. cream cheese
½ c. sugar
1 egg, beaten
1 tsp. vanilla
½ tsp. salt

Filling:
1½ c. brown sugar
¼ c. Therm-Flo
3 c. water
2 Tbsp. corn syrup
2 eggs, beaten
2 tsp. vanilla
6 Tbsp. butter

Crumbs:
1½ c. flour
½ c. brown sugar
½ tsp. soda

½ tsp. cream of tartar
½ c. butter, melted

Cream sugar and cream cheese together. Add egg, vanilla and salt. Put in bottom of 2 unbaked pie crusts. *For Filling*: Mix sugar and Therm-Flo together. Add water, corn syrup and eggs. Cook until thickened. Add vanilla and butter. Cool slightly, then pour on top of cream cheese mixture. *For Crumbs*: Mix all together and sprinkle on top. Bake at 350° for 35 minutes or until done.

144

Crumbs for Pies

MATTHIAS & NAOMI MAST

½ c. brown sugar
¾ c. flour
⅓ c. margarine
½ c. oatmeal

Mix together until crumbly. Use on top of rhubarb and apple pies.

Amish Crumb Pie

MARY LENGACHER

1 c. brown sugar
½ c. Karo
1 c. + 1 Tbsp. flour
1 egg, beaten
1 tsp. vanilla
¼ c. shortening
½ tsp. baking soda
½ tsp. baking powder
1 c. water

Combine ½ c. brown sugar, Karo, 1 Tbsp. flour, egg, 1 c. water and vanilla in saucepan and cook until thickened. Pour into a 9" unbaked pie crust. Mix together remaining flour, brown sugar, soda and baking powder. Cut in shortening until crumbly. Sprinkle on top of filling and bake at 350° until done, 30 minutes or so.

Coconut Pie

SAMUEL & LEANNA WEAVER

4 eggs
1¾ c. sugar
½ c. flour
¼ c. melted butter
2 c. milk
1½ c. coconut
1 tsp. vanilla

Combine ingredients in order given. Mix well. Pour into greased 10" pie pan. Bake at 350° for 45 minutes or until golden brown. The middle will appear rather soft. When done, it will have a delicate crust over the top. It will be solid enough to cut after cooled. Center is like cream pie–overbaking makes it more like cake. Rather "amazing" and simple. Recipe times 3 makes 4 pies (1 large & 3 small). Serves 8.

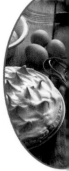

145

Coconut Oatmeal Custard Pie

JOHN & ESTA YODER

1 c. brown sugar
1 c. sugar
1 c. light Karo
4 tsp. flour
5 tsp. melted butter
6 eggs, separated
2¾ c. milk
1 can condensed milk
1 c. oatmeal
1 c. fine coconut
⅛ tsp. salt

Mix all ingredients, folding in beaten egg whites last. Bake at 400° for 10 minutes, then at 325° until done, around 45 minutes. Yield: 2 lg. pies.

Lemon Meringue Pie

LARRY & NAOMI LENGACHER

1 lemon, juice & rind
2 c. water
1 c. sugar
¼ tsp. salt
3 eggs, separated
4 Tbsp. cornstarch
1 Tbsp. butter

Meringue:
4 Tbsp. sugar
1 tsp. lemon juice
3 egg whites, beaten stiff

In a 6 qt. bowl or saucepan, mix cornstarch, sugar and salt; add water and egg yolks. Cook until thick. Add butter. If not enough lemon, add lemon flavor. I usually put topping on top of pie instead of meringue. Yield: 1 pie.

146

Chocolate Cream Pie

STEVIE & REBECCA SWAREY

3 c. milk
1¼ c. sugar
3 egg yolks
3 Tbsp. cornstarch
3 Tbsp. flour
1 c. brown sugar
⅓ c. cocoa
1½ tsp. vanilla
1½ Tbsp. butter
½ tsp. salt

Heat 2 c. milk with sugar and salt. Mix flour, cornstarch, brown sugar and egg yolks with 1 c. milk. Mix cocoa with hot water to make a paste. Pour all into hot milk and cook till thick; add vanilla and butter. This filling is enough for a 9"x13" pan delight or 1 large pie.

Dutch Apple Pie

VERNON & RUTH YODER

3 c. sliced or shredded apples
¾ c. sugar
½ c. water
1½ Tbsp. minute tapioca
pinch of salt
2 Tbsp. butter
¼-½ tsp. cinnamon

Bring first 5 ingredients to a boil. Remove from heat and add butter and cinnamon. Mix well and pour into a baked pie crust. Top with crumbs and bake at 350° till crumbs are lightly browned. Yield: 1 pie.

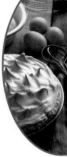

Crumbs:
½ c. oatmeal
½ c. flour
⅛ tsp. baking powder

¼ c. brown sugar
¼ c. butter, softened
⅛ tsp. cinnamon

Pies

Old-Fashioned Apple Pie

LUKE & KATHRYN MILLER

1 c. sugar
1 Tbsp. flour, heaping
2 tsp. clear jel, heaping
1 tsp. cinnamon
sliced apples

Mix first 4 ingredients together. Put half of mixture in unbaked pie shell. Slice apples in shell until heaping full. Put remaining mixture on top of apples. Dot with butter. Put crust on top. Brush with beaten egg or milk. Mix a little pie dough crumbs with sugar. Sprinkle on top. Bake at 400° until golden. Yield: 1 pie.

Shoofly Pie

STEVIE & REBECCA SWAREY

½ c. molasses
½ c. Karo
½ c. brown sugar
2 eggs
1 c. hot water
1 tsp. soda

Crumbs:
1 c. flour
½ c. brown sugar
¼ c. lard

Dissolve soda in hot water, mix together rest of ingredients. Add hot water and soda last. Beat. Pour half of syrup into an unbaked pie shell, top with half of crumbs, then rest of syrup, then top with rest of crumbs. Bake at 400° for 10 minutes, then at 350° for 40-50 minutes. Best served warm or cold with milk.

148

Rice Krispie Ice Cream Pie

MATTHIAS & NAOMI MAST

2 c. Rice Krispies
1 Tbsp. butter, melted
½ c. marshmallow creme

Chocolate Syrup:
¼ c. peanut butter
½ c. fudge or chocolate syrup
3 Tbsp. light Karo

Melt butter and blend with marshmallow creme. Add Rice Krispies and mix well. Put in greased pie pan and shape into crust. Chill. Fill crust with ice cream and freeze. Serve with fresh fruit filling or chocolate syrup. Melt together syrup ingredients.

Lemon Pie Filling

IVAN & BARBARA SCHLABACH

1¼ c. sugar
6 Tbsp. Therm-Flo
2 c. water
⅓ c. lemon juice
3 egg yolks
2½ Tbsp. butter
1½ tsp. lemon extract
2 tsp. vinegar

Combine first 5 ingredients. Cook until thick. Add rest of ingredients.

149

Blueberry Pie Filling

IVAN & BARBARA SCHLABACH

1 c. water
1 c. sugar
2½ c. blueberries
¼ c. Therm-Flo
¼ c. water
1½ tsp. lemon juice

Cook water, sugar and blueberries, then put through strainer. Thicken with Therm-Flo, water and lemon juice.

Pies

Cream Pie Filling

MATTHIAS & NAOMI MAST

For 1 pie
2 c. milk
½ c. sugar
2 Tbsp. clear jel
2 egg yolks
1 Tbsp. butter
½ tsp. salt
1 tsp. vanilla

For chocolate pie add:
¼ c. cocoa

For 4 pies:
8 c. milk
2 c. sugar
8 Tbsp. clear jel
8 egg yolks
8 Tbsp. butter
2 tsp. salt
2 tsp. vanilla

For 1 pie: Scald 1½ c. milk. Combine sugar, clear jel and salt. Stir in remaining ½ c. milk and egg yolks. Stir this mixture into scalded milk; cook until thickened. Remove from heat and add butter and vanilla. Cool with wax paper on top.

For 4 pies: Scald 6 c. milk. Combine sugar, clear jel and salt. Stir in remaining 2 c. milk and egg yolks. Stir into scalded milk. Remove from heat and add butter and vanilla. Cool with wax paper on top.

150

Desserts

Easy Custard

JAMES & IDA LEHMAN

½ gal. milk
12 eggs
1 Tbsp. flour, heaping
½ tsp. salt
1 c. sugar
1 c. brown sugar
1 tsp. vanilla

Heat milk in 3 qt. kettle until bubbly. Beat eggs and add rest of ingredients. Add mixture to hot milk. Pour into 9"x13" stainless steel cake pan. Bake at 475° for 5 minutes. Turn off oven. Leave set in oven until cool. Chill and enjoy. Serves 15.

Perfect Custard

LUKE & KATHRYN MILLER

½ gal. milk
12 eggs
1 Tbsp. flour, heaping
½ tsp. salt
1 c. sugar
1 c. brown sugar
1 tsp. vanilla

Heat milk till bubbly. Beat eggs. Add rest of ingredients. Add to hot milk. Pour into 9"x13" stainless steel cake pan. Bake at 475° for 3 minutes. Turn off heat. Let set in oven till cold.

Note: Be sure to use stainless steel cake pan.

152

Strawberry Dessert Topping

MATTHIAS & NAOMI MAST

1 qt. frozen strawberries, blended
1½ c. water
⅓ c. clear jel
1 c. sugar

Mix water, sugar and clear jel in saucepan, cook until thickened. Blend in with strawberries. Tastes like fresh strawberry filling. Use on top of cakes, cheesecakes or fruit pizza. Also delicious in yogurt.

Fruit Dessert

ATLEE & MATTIE MILLER

⅔ c. instant vanilla pudding
1½ c. pineapple juice
2 cans pineapple tidbits
4 oz. cream cheese, softened
12 oz. Cool Whip
11 oz. mandarin oranges
2 c. purple grapes
1 bag sm. marshmallows

Drain pineapple; add water to make 1½ c. for pudding mixture. Add cream cheese and topping and cool till set. Add rest of fruit, etc.

Fruit Glaze

MATTHIAS & NAOMI MAST

juice from 1 can pineapples,
    then add water to make 3 c.
1½ c. sugar
pinch of salt
1 sm. box lemon Jell-O or ⅓ c.
¼ c. ReaLemon
½ c. clear jel
¾ c. water

In a saucepan mix first 3 ingredients and bring to a boil. Mix clear jel and water and stir into boiling mixture. Stir until thickened, remove from heat and add Jell-O and lemon juice. Cool and add your favorite fruit.

153

Desserts

Fruit Pizza

MATTHIAS & NAOMI MAST

Crust:
½ c. butter
½ c. cane sugar
1 egg
1⅓ c. flour
1 tsp. baking powder
pinch of salt

Filling:
8 oz. cream cheese
½ c. powdered sugar
½ tsp. vanilla
1½ c. whipped topping

Glaze if using fresh fruit:
2 c. pineapple juice
½ c. cane sugar

1 Tbsp. clear jel, heaping
2 Tbsp. lemon or pineapple
   Jell-O

Cream together butter and sugar; add egg; blend in flour, baking powder and salt. Press into greased 11"x17" pan. Bake at 375° for 10 minutes. If you happen to overbake a little, top right away with filling and refrigerate and it will soften. Cream together filling ingredients. Top with fresh fruit and glaze or pie filling of your choice.

154

12-Layer Salad

MARY LENGACHER

6 (3 oz.) pkg. Jell-O,
  any flavor—I usually use
  2 orange, 2 raspberry, 2 lime
16 oz. sour cream, softened

Add 1 c. boiling water to 1 pkg. Jell-O. Take out half and add ⅓ c. sour cream, slowly, and mix well. Pour into 9"x13" pan, chill till firm. Meanwhile, add 3 Tbsp. cold water to remaining ½ c. Jell-O. Pour on top of first layer, chill again till firm. Repeat with other flavors, making sure Jell-Os are cool enough to pour on the other layers. Cut into squares. It looks pretty in a glass cake pan.

Note: It takes several hours or more to make, till the last layer is on. This is a favorite of ours, especially for holidays.

Creamy Quick Salad

MARY LENGACHER

8 oz. Cool Whip
16 oz. sm. curd cottage cheese
⅓ c. orange Jell-O
10 oz. crushed pineapple, drained
11 oz. mandarin oranges, drained

Fold Cool Whip, cottage cheese and Jell-O together. Add fruit. Refrigerate several hours before serving.

Cherry Coke Salad

MATTHEW & MARLENE TROYER

1 (20 oz.) can crushed pineapple
½ c. water
⅔ c. cherry Jell-O
1 (21 oz.) can cherry pie filling
¾ c. cherry Coke

Drain pineapple, reserving juice (set fruit aside). In a saucepan or microwave, bring pineapple juice and water to a boil. Add Jell-O, stir until dissolved. Stir in pie filling and Coke. Pour into serving bowl. Refrigerate until slightly thickened, fold in pineapple. Refrigerate until firm. This is delicious with whipped topping. Serves 10.

Blueberry, Raspberry Pudding Cake

STEVIE & REBECCA SWAREY

1½ c. blueberries
1½ c. raspberries
1 c. flour
1 tsp. baking powder
¼ tsp. salt
1½ c. sugar
½ c. milk
3 Tbsp. butter, melted
1 tsp. vanilla
1 Tbsp. cornstarch
1 c. boiling water

Preheat oven to 350°. Place fruit in bottom of a buttered 9" or 10" round cake pan. Combine flour, baking powder, salt and half the sugar in a mixing bowl. Add milk, butter and vanilla. Beat till smooth. Spread batter over fruit. Combine remaining sugar and cornstarch and sprinkle over batter and pour boiling water over mixture. Bake 45 minutes. Serve warm with ice cream or milk.

156

Fruit Cobbler

SAMUEL & LEANNA WEAVER

1 qt. fresh fruit
1 c. evaporated cane juice/sugar
2 c. flour
2 c. sugar
3 tsp. baking powder
2 tsp. salt
1½ c. milk

Mix fruit and sugar. Let set. Put ¼ c. butter in 9"x13" pan and allow to melt in oven while it heats to 375°. Mix batter. Put fruit in pan. Put batter over all and bake for 45 minutes. Serve warm with milk or ice cream. Serves 10.

If we have this as a 1 dish meal, 5 boys will make it disappear fast! Especially with peaches! A pie filling such as cherry works, too.

Crunchy Cobbler Topping

STEVIE & REBECCA SWAREY

1 c. sugar
1 c. flour
1 tsp. baking powder
1 tsp. salt
⅓ c. cold butter
1 egg, beaten

Combine dry ingredients. Cut in cold butter until mixture resembles fine crumbs. Stir in egg. Bake at 375° for 35 to 40 minutes or till filling is bubbly and top is brown. This is delicious with peaches or can be used with whatever fruit. Our favorite!

157

Strawberry Tapioca

JAMES & IDA LEHMAN

9 c. water
1 tsp. salt
1½ c. baby pearl tapioca
1 c. strawberry Jell-O
⅔ c. raspberry Jell-O
½ gal. vanilla ice cream
1 qt. strawberries

Bring water and salt to a boil and add tapioca. Turn off heat and let set for 35 minutes. Bring to a boil again and add Jell-Os. Take off heat and cool. Just before serving, add ice cream and strawberries. Do not overmix. Very refreshing on a warm summer day. Serves 25.

Fluffy Tapioca Pudding

LUKE & KATHRYN MILLER

3 Tbsp. minute tapioca
3 Tbsp. sugar
1 egg yolk
2 Tbsp. sugar
⅛ tsp. salt
2 c. milk
1 egg white
¾ tsp. vanilla

Mix tapioca, salt, 3 Tbsp. sugar, milk and egg yolk in saucepan. Let set for 5 minutes. Cook over medium heat to a full boil. Beat egg white. Gradually add 2 Tbsp. sugar, beating till stiff peaks form. Add to tapioca. Stir in vanilla.

Vanilla Pudding

ENOS & NANCY TROYER

8 c. milk
2¾ c. sugar
1 c. cornstarch, heaping
½ tsp. salt
6 egg yolks, beaten
milk to mix well
2 Tbsp. butter
1 tsp. vanilla

While 8 c. milk is brought to boiling, mix cornstarch, sugar and salt. Then add beaten eggs and enough milk to make mixing easy. Pour into hot milk and keep boiling and stirring till thickened. Add butter and vanilla once removed from heat. I use this for coconut cream pie, peanut butter pie or graham cracker pudding. Yummy and easy. Serves 7.

Chocolate Cake Pudding

SAMUEL & LEANNA WEAVER

1½ c. evaporated cane juice
2 c. Prairie Gold flour
½ tsp. salt
4 tsp. baking powder
¼ c. baking cocoa
6 Tbsp. melted butter or oil
2 tsp. vanilla
1 c. milk

Mix dry ingredients; add milk, butter and vanilla. Bake at 350° for 45 minutes. *Topping:* Mix and sprinkle over top and pour 3½ c. water over all. Serves 10.

159

Topping:
2 c. sugar (1 c. Sucanut &
   1 c. evaporated cane juice)

½ c. baking cocoa

Triple Orange Pudding

MATTHIAS & NAOMI MAST

1 box orange Jell-O
1 box vanilla pudding
1 box tapioca pudding
2½ c. water
1 can mandarin oranges
2 c. Cool Whip

Combine Jell-O, puddings and water to a boil, remove from heat and cool. When cooled add Cool Whip and oranges.

Homemade Yogurt

SAMUEL & LEANNA WEAVER

1 gal. milk
2 c. sugar or
  evaporated cane juice
2 Tbsp. gelatin,
  dissolved in cold water
4 Tbsp. yogurt/starter
2 Tbsp. vanilla

160

Heat milk to 190°. Add sugar and gelatin. Cool to 130°; add yogurt and vanilla. Whip up well with whisk. Put in warm place overnight or for the day. A dehydrator at 115° for 10 hours works well. You may stir in pie filling for flavor.

Baked Apples

LUKE & KATHRYN MILLER

1 c. sugar
¼ c. clear jel
1 tsp. cinnamon
1 c. brown sugar
2 c. water
2 tsp. butter
¼ tsp. salt
6 med. apples, peeled & halved

Boil first 7 ingredients together and pour over apples that have been peeled and placed in a 9"x13" pan. Bake at 350° for 30-40 minutes or until apples are soft. Delicious served warm with ice cream.

Baked Caramel Apples

JUSTIN & NAOMI MILLER

2 Tbsp. clear jel
1 c. water
1 c. brown sugar
2 c. boiling water
¼ tsp. salt
2 Tbsp. butter
1 tsp. vanilla
9 apples, pared & peeled

Mix clear jel with a small amount of water. Add rest of water, sugar, butter, salt and vanilla. Heat, stirring constantly till thickened. Place apple halves in a baking dish side by side and pour sauce over apples. Bake at 400° for 30-35 minutes. Serve warm with whipped topping or ice cream.

Pumpkin Roll

JACOB & LORETTA WEAVER

1 c. pumpkin or squash
1 c. sugar
1 tsp. lemon juice
1 tsp. baking powder
2 tsp. cinnamon
1 tsp. ginger
½ tsp. nutmeg
½ tsp. salt
¾ c. flour
3 eggs

Filling:
8 oz. cream cheese, softened
¼ c. butter or margarine

1 c. powdered sugar
1 tsp. vanilla

Beat eggs until thick, about 5 minutes. Add other ingredients and mix well. Spread in 10"x15" pan, lined with waxed paper. Bake at 300°-325° until done. Turn onto paper towels sprinkled with powdered sugar. Roll up with towel and cool. Mix filling ingredients. Unroll and spread with filling; reroll (without towel of course) and refrigerate. Slice when chilled.

161

Peter Pumpkin

JOSEPH & RHODA MILLER

1 pt. pumpkin
12 oz. milk
3 eggs, beaten
1 c. sugar
½ c. brown sugar
1 tsp. cinnamon
½ tsp. salt

Put in a 9"x13" pan and sprinkle yellow cake mix on top. Melt 1 c. butter and pour over cake mix. Bake at 350° for approx. 1 hour. Serve with ice cream while warm. Serves 10. Delicious!

Pumpkin Torte

MATTHIAS & NAOMI MAST

162

24 graham crackers
⅓ c. sugar
½ c. butter
2 eggs, beaten
¼ c. sugar
8 oz. cream cheese
2 c. pumpkin
3 eggs, separated
½ c. sugar
1 Tbsp. gelatin
¼ c. cold water
½ c. milk
½ tsp. salt
1 Tbsp. cinnamon
8 oz. whipped topping

Mix together graham crackers, ⅓ c. sugar and butter and press into 9"x13" pan. Then mix together 2 eggs, ¼ c. sugar and cream cheese and pour over crust; bake at 350° for 20 minutes. Cook pumpkin, egg yolks, ½ c. sugar, milk, salt and cinnamon until mixture thickens. Remove from heat and add gelatin dissolved in cold water. Cool. Beat egg whites and ¼ c. sugar, fold into pumpkin mixture. Add 1 c. whipped topping. Pour over cooled crust. Top with rest of whipped topping.

Butternut Squash Bake

MATTHEW & MARLENE TROYER

⅓ c. butter, softened
¾ c. sugar
2 eggs
5 oz. evaporated milk
1 tsp. vanilla
2 c. cooked & mashed squash
½ c. Rice Krispies
¼ c. brown sugar
¼-½ c. pecans
2 Tbsp. butter

Mix first 6 ingredients and put into a 9"x13" baking dish. For topping, mix last 4 ingredients and put on top of first mixture. Bake at 350° for 45 minutes. This is delicious with whipped topping. Serves 10.

Cream Puff Dessert

MICHAEL & JOANNE COBLENTZ

1 c. water
½ c. butter
1 c. flour
4 eggs

Filling:
3½ c. milk
2 (3 oz.) pkg. instant vanilla pudding
8 oz. cream cheese

Topping:
whipped topping
chocolate or caramel syrup

Bring water and butter to a rolling boil. Add flour all at one time and mix well. Add eggs one at a time and mix well. Put into greased 9"x13" pan. Bake at 400° for 30-35 minutes. Mix pudding with milk and mix with cream cheese. Pour into crust and top with whipped topping. Just before serving, drizzle chocolate or caramel topping on top. Delicious!

163

Zucchini Cobbler

ED & MARY SLABAUGH

8 c. chopped, seeded & peeled
zucchini
⅔ c. lemon juice
1 c. sugar
1 tsp. cinnamon
½ tsp. nutmeg

Crust:
4 c. all-purpose flour
2 c. sugar
1½ c. cold butter
1 tsp. cinnamon

In a large saucepan, over medium heat, cook and stir zucchini and lemon juice for 15-20 minutes or until zucchini is tender. Add sugar, cinnamon and nutmeg. Simmer 1 minute longer. Remove from heat and set aside. *Crust:* Combine flour and sugar in a bowl; cut in butter until mixture resembles coarse crumbs. Stir ½ c. into zucchini mixture. Press half of remaining crumb mixture into a greased 15"x10"x1" baking pan. Spread zucchini over top; crumble remaining crust mixture over zucchini. Sprinkle with cinnamon. Bake at 375° for 35-40 minutes. Serves 16-20.

Note: This is my surprise dessert! No one guesses the "secret ingredient" is zucchini.

Rhubarb Dessert

STEVIE & REBECCA SWAREY

8 c. rhubarb
6 oz. strawberry Jell-O
1½ c. sugar
1 box yellow cake mix
⅔ c. butter, melted

Mix together first 3 ingredients and put in a 9"x13" pan. Sprinkle yellow cake mix over top, then drizzle melted butter over cake mix. Bake at 375° for 40-50 minutes. Serve warm with milk or ice cream.

Yummy Dessert

ATLEE & MATTIE MILLER

Crust:
1 c. flour
½ c. butter
¼ c. nuts
2 tsp. brown sugar

Layer 1:
8 oz. cream cheese, softened
1 c. powdered sugar
½ c. peanut butter
8 oz. Cool Whip

Layer 2:
1 pkg. vanilla instant pudding   3 c. milk
1 pkg. chocolate instant pudding

Last Layer:
8 oz. Cool Whip   Hershey bar, crushed

Mix first 4 ingredients and press into a (9" x 13") glass pan. Bake at 350° for 10-12 minutes. Cool. Mix next 4 ingredients together and whip till smooth; add on crust. Chill before adding layer 2. Whip pudding and milk together, pour on first layer. When cold and set add last layer. Enjoy! Serves 20.

165

Double Chocolate Mocha Trifle

MATTHIAS & NAOMI MAST

1 brownie mix or cake mix
2 pkg. white chocolate instant pudding
1¾ c. cold milk
4 tsp. instant coffee
¼ c. warm water
2 c. whipped cream or ice cream
3 toffee bars, shredded

Mix brownie or cake mix according to directions and bake. Cut into 1" squares. Mix pudding with milk. Dissolve coffee in warm water and add to pudding; add 2 c. whipped cream or ice cream. Spread cake on platter and top with pudding mixture and shredded toffee bars.

Desserts

Triple Berry Trifle

MATTHIAS & NAOMI MAST

½ angel food cake
1 box instant pudding
1 c. milk
1 c. sour cream or ice cream
8 oz. Cool Whip

Cut angel food cake into 1" pieces, spread on platter. In bowl, mix pudding with milk and beat; add ice cream or sour cream and Cool Whip. Top with 1 c. fresh strawberries, 1 c. raspberries and ¾ c. blueberries.

Mini Mocha Cheesecakes

IVAN & BARBARA SCHLABACH

166

1½ c. graham cracker crumbs
¼ c. sugar
⅓ c. butter, melted
3 (8 oz.) pkg. cream cheese
3 eggs
1 Tbsp. instant coffee, heaping
2 Tbsp. hot water
  (mix with coffee)
⅓ c. Ovaltine chocolate malt
1 tsp. vanilla
1 (14 oz.) can sweetened
  condensed milk

Mix first 3 ingredients together. Put 1¾ Tbsp. crumbs into cupcake liners. Pack lightly. Whip cream cheese until creamy. Add rest of ingredients. Mix well. Fill cupcake liners about ¾ full. Bake at 325° for approx. 30 minutes. Cool. Put a dab of Cool Whip on top. They freeze well. Yield: 21.

S'mores Cheesecake

STEVIE & REBECCA SWAREY

Crust:
2¼ c. graham cracker crumbs
⅓ c. sugar
½ c. butter, melted

Filling:
2 (8 oz.) pkg. cream cheese
1 c. condensed milk
2 tsp. vanilla
3 eggs
1 c. chocolate chips
miniature marshmallows

For Crust: Mix ingredients and press in a springform pan. *For Filling:* Beat first 3 ingredients till smooth. Add eggs, beat again. Stir in chocolate chips. Bake at 325° for 40-45 minutes, till center is almost set. Sprinkle with miniature marshmallows. Bake 4-6 minutes longer. Melt ½ c. chocolate chips with 1 Tbsp. butter and drizzle over top. Yummy!

Frozen Cheesecake

ATLEE & MATTIE MILLER

Crust:
1 pkg. graham crackers, crushed
2 Tbsp. brown sugar
¼ c. butter, browned

Filling:
2 (8 oz.) cream cheese, softened
1 can condensed milk
1 tsp. vanilla
2 c. Rich's topping, whipped

Glaze:
2 c. water
1 c. sugar
⅓ c. Fridgex

Freeze crust in a 9"x13" pan. Add cream cheese mixture. *For Glaze:* Cook ingredients together, add strawberry Kool-Aid, flavor of your choice. Cool.

Note: I like to swirl the glaze into the whipped mixture and freeze. Ready to serve after frozen then.

167

Desserts

Frozen Strawberry Fluff

MATTHIAS & NAOMI MAST

8 oz. cream cheese
¾ c. sugar
16 oz. Cool Whip
1 can crushed pineapple,
  undrained
1 qt. chopped thawed
  strawberries
3-5 bananas

Beat cream cheese with sugar. Add Cool Whip. Slowly add pineapple, strawberries and bananas. Pour into a 9"x13" pan and freeze.

Raspberry Fluff

MATTHIAS & NAOMI MAST

1 qt. or tube raspberry pie filling
1 can Eagle Brand milk
12 oz. Cool Whip
8 oz. crushed pineapple,
  undrained (optional)

Mix together and freeze. Good if partly thawed before serving.

168

Oreo Cookie Delight

STEVE & MIRIAM LENGACHER

2 c. powdered sugar
8 oz. cream cheese
1 c. peanut butter
1 c. milk
16 oz. Cool Whip
22 Oreo cookies

Beat sugar, cream cheese and peanut butter. Blend in milk, then fold in Cool Whip. Crumble 11 cookies on bottom of a 9"x13" pan. Pour mixture on crumbs, crumble 11 more cookies on top. Freeze.

Frozen Orange Slush

LUKE & KATHRYN MILLER

3 c. warm water
2 c. sugar
1 (16 oz.) can frozen orange
 juice
1 (20 oz.) can fruit cocktail
8 bananas, sliced
1 qt. peaches

Mix together. Pour into containers and freeze. Yield: 4 qts.

Strawberry Yum-Yum

JOSIAH & RHODA MILLER

1 c. flour
½ c. butter
¼ c. brown sugar
½ c. chopped nuts
2 egg whites
2 tsp. lemon juice
1 c. sugar
2-2½ c. strawberries, frozen
8 oz. Cool Whip

Mix the first 4 ingredients until crumbly and press into 8"x8" pan. Bake at 350° for 20-25 minutes. Cool and break into crumbs. Place crumbs in a 9"x13" pan, saving some for top; set aside. Beat egg whites with sugar and lemon juice until stiff. Add strawberries and Cool Whip. Spread strawberry mixture over crumbs and put remaining crumbs on top. Freeze. Serve frozen.

169

Note: Make 2 batches crumbs and 3 batches filling for large cake taker.

Desserts

Drumstick Dessert

CHERYL ANNE YODER

Crust:
1½ c. graham cracker crumbs, about 24 squares
½ c. chopped, salted peanuts
¼ c. butter, melted
2 Tbsp. peanut butter

Filling:
1 pkg. cream cheese
½ c. sugar
½ c. peanut butter
1-2 tsp. vanilla
4 eggs
16 oz. Cool Whip

½-1 c. Hershey's syrup

For Crust: Mix ingredients; press in a 9"x13" pan. Reserve half for topping. Put in freezer till solid. *For Filling:* Beat cream cheese and sugar. Mix in peanut butter and vanilla; add beaten eggs. Fold in Cool Whip. Spread cream cheese mixture over crust. Drizzle Hershey's syrup over top. Sprinkle remaining crumbs on top. Freeze overnight or a few hours. Remove from freezer 15 minutes before serving. Keeps well in freezer for 3 months. Very good!

Frosty Pumpkin Dessert

JOHN & ESTA YODER

3 c. graham cracker crumbs
1 c. melted butter
¼ c. sugar

Filling:
2 c. canned pumpkin
½ c. brown sugar
1 tsp. salt
1 tsp. cinnamon
1 tsp. ginger
2 qt. vanilla ice cream
½ c. chopped walnuts (optional)

Combine cracker crumbs, sugar and butter. Reserve about ¾ c. crumbs for topping. Press remaining crumbs into buttered 9"x13" pan. Chill. Mix filling ingredients together and stir in softened ice cream and nuts. Put on top of crumb layer. Sprinkle remaining crumbs on top. Freeze.

Ice Cream Pudding

EMILY RUTH YODER (AGE 8)

2 stacks Ritz or Townhouse
  crackers
½ c. butter
1 c. chopped nuts
1 pkg. instant vanilla pudding
1 pkg. instant coconut cream
  pudding
1½ c. milk
1 qt. vanilla ice cream, softened

Melt butter; add crushed crackers and nuts. Put in bottom of a 9"x13" pan. Mix together puddings and milk and add to softened ice cream. Pour on top of crust and freeze.

Ice Cream Brownie Dessert

JAY & AMY TROYER

brownies
ice cream
Cool Whip
Nesquik
chocolate syrup

Place brownies in bottom of pan. Put ice cream on top. Mix Nesquik with Cool Whip and put on top of ice cream. Garnish with chocolate syrup. Enjoy!

171

Oreo Ice Cream Dessert

MICHAEL & JOANNE COBLENTZ

16 oz. Oreo cookies
¼ c. butter, melted
½ gal. vanilla ice cream
chocolate syrup
8 oz. Cool Whip

Crush cookies and mix with butter. Reserve some crumbs for top. Press rest of crumbs in a 9"x13" pan. Top with ice cream. Spread chocolate syrup on top of ice cream. Spoon Cool Whip over syrup and spread evenly. Top with cookie crumbs. Very simple and delicious.

Homemade Ice Cream

MICHAEL & JOANNE COBLENTZ

2 qt. milk
1 c. sugar
1 c. brown sugar
1 Tbsp. vanilla
¼ tsp. salt
1 tsp. plain gelatin
¼ c. cold water
6 eggs
1 can Eagle Brand milk
3 c. whipped topping

Heat milk until scalded. Add sugar, vanilla and salt. Dissolve gelatin in water and add to milk mixture. Cool. Beat eggs well. Add eggs, milk and whipped topping and mix all together. Freeze. Yield: 1½ gal.

Dairy Queen Ice Cream

MATTHIAS & NAOMI MAST

2 Tbsp. gelatin
½ c. water
5 c. milk
2 c. sugar
2 tsp. vanilla
1 tsp. salt
2 c. cream

Soak gelatin in water. Heat milk, but not boiling. (If you pour sugar in the milk but do not stir, it will not burn.) Remove from heat. Add gelatin, sugar, vanilla and salt. Cool; add cream. Yield: 1 gal. Freeze in ice cream freezer. *Variation:* Chocolate Dairy Queen Ice Cream: Mix together 3 Tbsp. cocoa and ½ c. extra sugar. Heat with milk. Proceed same as vanilla flavor. This gets very fluffy.

172

Our Favorite Ice Cream

JUSTIN & NAOMI MILLER

4 eggs, beaten
½ c. brown sugar
1 can evaporated milk
½ c. corn syrup
1 tsp. vanilla
1 can Eagle Brand milk
2 tsp. maple flavoring
pinch of salt
4 c. milk
3 oz. vanilla pudding
2 c. whipped topping

Mix all ingredients well. Pour into a 4 qt. freezer and freeze.

Ice Cream

MATTHEW & MARLENE TROYER

8 c. milk
2½ c. sugar
8 egg yolks
4 Tbsp. cornstarch
1 tsp. salt
4 tsp. vanilla
12 oz. Cool Whip
8 egg whites, beaten

Mix sugar and cornstarch. Add egg yolks and 3 c. milk. Heat rest of milk in 8 qt. kettle. Add sugar and cornstarch mixture. Bring to a boil, stirring constantly. Remove from heat. Add salt, vanilla and beaten egg whites. Cool completely. Put Cool Whip in bottom of 6 qt. freezer. Add pudding mixture and freeze.

173

Strawberry Cheesecake Ice Cream

STEVIE & REBECCA SWAREY

4 c. sugar
5 Tbsp. cornstarch
pinch of salt
10 c. milk
6 eggs, lightly beaten
8 oz. cream cheese
1 Tbsp. vanilla
2 c. heavy cream

Bring 8 c. milk to a boil. Mix sugar, cornstarch and salt to rest of the milk. Stir into boiling milk and cook and stir till thickened. Beat eggs, add ½ c. milk and whisk into mixture, stirring constantly. Cook and stir over low heat till mixture reaches at least 160° and coats the back of metal spoon. Remove from heat. Stir in cream cheese until melted. Add vanilla and refrigerate a couple hours or overnight. Pour into 1½ qt. freezer and add cream and milk till ⅔ full. Top with strawberries when frozen.

174

Coffee Ice Cream

MATTHIAS & NAOMI MAST

1 qt. half and half
1 pt. whipping cream
1½ Tbsp. vanilla
1½ c. sugar
1 can sweetened condensed milk
1 sm. box instant vanilla pudding
⅔ bag crushed Heath bars
dash of salt
¾ c. instant coffee

Whip whipping cream, then add rest of ingredients except for Heath bars. Pour into 6 qt. freezer. Add whole milk to 5-6 inches from top of can. Start freezing. When ice cream is about half done, add Heath bars.

Hot Fudge Sauce

MATTHIAS & NAOMI MAST

1 c. sugar
⅓ c. cocoa
2 Tbsp. flour
¼ tsp. salt
1 c. water
1 Tbsp. butter
½ tsp. vanilla

Mix all together in saucepan. Cook until thickened.

Ice Cream Topping

SAMUEL & LEANNA WEAVER

2 c. chocolate chips
½ c. butter
⅓ c. peanut butter

Melt together and cool. Then serve on ice cream; will harden on ice cream. Do not refrigerate.

175

Other Favorite Desserts

RECIPE FOR _____

_____

_____

_____

_____

_____

_____

_____

_____

_____

_____

_____

_____

RECIPE FOR _____

_____

_____

_____

_____

_____

_____

_____

_____

_____

_____

_____

_____

Cakes and Frostings

Sugar-Free Hawaiian Cake

MATTHEW & MARLENE TROYER

2 c. wheat flour

2 tsp. soda

1 c. chopped nuts

¾ c. honey

1 c. coconut

1 tsp. vanilla

1 (20 oz.) can crushed pineapple, with juice

Topping:

8 oz. cream cheese

½ c. coconut

¼ c. butter

½ c. nuts

maple syrup

Mix cake ingredients and bake in a Bundt pan at 350° till done. When cool, mix topping ingredients and put on cake which has been taken out of pan. One of our favorites!

Ruby Troyer Pineapple Cake

ENOS & NANCY TROYER

2 c. sugar

2 eggs

2 tsp. soda

2 c. flour

1 (20 oz.) can crushed pineapple

Dump everything into bowl at once and stir. Bake at 350° in a 9"x13" pan. A moist cake and good with cream cheese frosting.

Pineapple Cake

STEVIE & REBECCA SWAREY

2 eggs
2 c. flour
2 c. sugar
1 tsp. vanilla
¼ tsp. salt
1 (20 oz.) can crushed pineapple

Mix together first 5 ingredients, then add pineapple. Bake 25-30 minutes in a 9"x13" pan or a sheet pan. Frost with cream cheese frosting. Can also use for a delight bottom, with cream cheese and whipped topping center, then top with crushed pineapples, thickened with sugar and cornstarch.

For the pineapple lovers.

Pineapple Cake

JACOB & LORETTA WEAVER

2 c. flour
2 c. sugar
2 tsp. soda
2 eggs
1 can crushed pineapple,
   undrained

Mix well. Bake at 350°. Frost with cream cheese frosting. Store in refrigerator. Enjoy!

179

Cakes & Frostings

Orange Juice Cake

MATTHEW & MARLENE TROYER, ENOS & NANCY TROYER

yellow cake mix
½ c. vegetable oil
4 eggs
1 box vanilla pudding
1 c. orange juice, diluted

Sauce:
½ c. butter
1 c. orange juice
1 c. sugar

Mix and put in well greased Bundt pan. Bake at 350° for 45-50 minutes. While cake is still hot pour sauce over top (that has been boiled for 3 minutes). Let cake set for 30-45 minutes, then take out of pan. Serves 12.

Banana Cake

VERNON & RUTH YODER

½ c. butter
2 eggs
2 c. flour
½ tsp. salt
1 c. sugar
1 c. bananas, mashed
1 tsp. soda
½ c. instant vanilla pudding

Cream butter and sugar; add eggs, soda, bananas, instant pudding and salt. Stir in flour. Put in a 9"x13" pan and top with crumbs. Bake at 350° for 30-35 minutes or until done.

Crumbs:
6 Tbsp. sugar
4 Tbsp. flour

2 Tbsp. melted butter

180

White Cake

MATTHIAS & NAOMI MAST

½ c. butter, softened
1 c. cold water
3 c. cake flour
1½ c. sugar
4 tsp. baking powder
4 egg whites

Combine all ingredient, adding egg whites last. Bake at 350° till golden brown.

Pumpkin Spice Cake

JAMES & IDA LEHMAN

2 c. flour
2 c. sugar
2 tsp. baking powder
2 tsp. soda
½ tsp. salt
2 tsp. cinnamon
2 c. pumpkin
4 eggs
1 c. salad oil
1 c. nuts

Mix dry ingredients. Add remaining ingredients, except nuts. Beat until smooth. Add nuts. Pour into a 9"x13" pan. Bake at 350° for 45 minutes. Serves 18.

181

Frosting:
½ c. butter
8 oz. cream cheese

1 tsp. vanilla
3 c. powdered sugar

Apple Cake

JAMES & IDA LEHMAN

1 c. sugar
½ c. shortening
2 eggs
1½ c. flour
1 tsp. soda
1 tsp. cinnamon
1 tsp. salt
1 tsp. vanilla
3 apples, shredded

Mix ingredients. Spread in a 9"x13" pan and sprinkle topping over cake. Bake at 350° for 40-45 minutes. Serve warm with whipped topping. Serves 18.

Topping:
1 Tbsp. butter
½ c. brown sugar

2 Tbsp. flour
½ c. chopped nuts

Oatmeal Cake

VERNON & RUTH YODER

1½ c. boiling water
1 c. quick oats
½ c. olive oil
1 c. sugar
1 c. brown sugar
2 eggs, beaten well
1½ c. flour
1 tsp. baking soda
½ tsp. salt
½ tsp. cinnamon

Stir together boiling water and quick oats. Let set for 20 minutes. Mix rest of ingredients, add oatmeal mixture and mix well. Bake in a 9"x13" pan at 350°.

182

Oatmeal Cake Frosting

VERNON & RUTH YODER

1 c. brown sugar
4 Tbsp. milk
2 Tbsp. butter
2 Tbsp. flour
nuts
coconut

Bring brown sugar, milk and butter to a boil. Add rest of ingredients. Spread over oatmeal cake. Toast in broiler till lightly browned. Do not burn!

Ruth's Oatmeal Cake

ED & MARY SLABAUGH

1½ c. boiling water
1 c. quick oats
¼ c. butter, softened
1 c. brown sugar
1 c. sugar
2 eggs
1 tsp. vanilla
1⅓ c. flour
1 tsp. soda
1 tsp. salt
1 tsp. cinnamon

Pour boiling water over oats and let set for 20 minutes. Cream together butter, sugars and eggs. Add the oatmeal and rest of dry ingredients. Bake at 350° approx. 30 minutes. Remove from oven and pour on the topping. Then put in broiler a few minutes.

183

Topping:

⅓ c. melted shortening or butter
½ c. brown sugar
½ tsp. vanilla

½ c. nuts
¼ c. milk
1 c. coconut

Watergate Cake

ED & MARY SLABAUGH

1 white cake mix
⅓ c. vegetable oil
3 eggs
½ c. chopped pecans
1 c. ginger ale
½ c. instant pistachio pudding
⅔ c. water

Mix cake ingredients and bake at temperature on cake box. *Frosting:* Beat topping until it forms stiff peaks. Mix milk and pudding mix, then fold into topping. Serves 20.

Frosting:
1 c. Rich's topping
1½ c. milk

½ c. dry instant pistachio pudding

184

Ozark Mountain Apple Cake

SAMUEL & LEANNA WEAVER

½ c. shortening
2 c. sugar
2 tsp. cinnamon
2 eggs
1 tsp. salt
2 tsp. soda
2 c. flour
4 c. chopped apples
2 tsp. vanilla

Cream sugar and shortening. Add well beaten eggs. Sift dry ingredients together. Stir in all with apples and vanilla. Pour into greased 9"x13" pan. Bake at 350° for 40-50 minutes. *Topping:* Combine ingredients in saucepan, bring to a boil. Pour sauce over top of cake. Good warm, with ice cream.

Ozark Topping:
½ c. brown sugar
½ c. sugar
½ tsp. vanilla

½ c. butter
½ c. cream

Yummy Coffee Cake

1 yellow cake mix
¾ c. vanilla instant pudding
4 eggs
1 tsp. vanilla
½ tsp. cinnamon
8 oz. sour cream
½ c. cooking oil
½ c. water

Put half of batter in bottom of a greased 9"x13" cake pan. Sprinkle with ½ of sugar mixture. Add rest of batter and sprinkle with rest of sugar mixture. Take knife through batter to make swirls. Bake at 350° for 30-40 minutes.

Sugar Mixture:
⅓ c. sugar
⅓ c. brown sugar

⅔ c. chopped pecans

Rich Strawberry Shortcakes

ENOS & NANCY TROYER

2 c. flour
2 Tbsp. sugar
4 tsp. baking powder
½ tsp. salt
½ c. butter, softened
1 egg, beaten
½ c. light cream
soft butter
4 c. sweetened sliced or chopped
  strawberries
whipped cream or ice cream

185

Sift together flour, sugar, baking powder and salt. Cut in butter till crumbly. Combine egg and cream/milk; add to flour mixture, stirring just until dough follows fork around bowl. On lightly floured surface, roll out to ½" thickness. Cut with a 2½" round cutter. Bake on ungreased sheets at 450° about 8 minutes. Split biscuits, spread with butter and spoon berries over them. Serve warm. Milk, ice cream or whipped topping over them is good, or plain. Serves 6.

Cakes & Frostings

Chocolate Mocha Cake

JUSTIN & NAOMI MILLER, STEVIE & REBECCA SWAREY

1 chocolate cake mix

Crumbs:
1½ c. graham crackers
¾ c. brown sugar
½ c. melted butter
1 tsp. instant coffee

Mix cake mix as directed on box. Put crumbs on bottom of cake pan. Top with chocolate cake. Bake at 350° till done. Cool. Top with topping.

Topping:
8 oz. Cool Whip or Rich's topping
8 oz. cream cheese
½ c. powdered sugar
1 Tbsp. instant coffee or Nesquik

Honduras Chocolate Cake

ENOS & NANCY TROYER

186

4 eggs
2 c. lard or butter
2 c. sour milk
4 tsp. vanilla
4 c. sugar
1⅓ c. baking cocoa
6½ c. flour
4 tsp. soda
2 tsp. salt
2 c. hot water

Mix first 5 ingredients together. Then mix next 4 ingredients together in separate bowl. Mix with first mixture, whipping it up well. Last add the hot water. Bake at 325° for 50 minutes. This is enough for 2 (9"x13") pans.

Verba's Famous Chocolate Cake

MATTHEW & MARLENE TROYER

2½ c. brown sugar
3 c. flour
½ c. butter
1 c. buttermilk
1 c. boiling water
2 eggs
2 tsp. soda
2 tsp. baking powder
½ c. cocoa
1 tsp. vanilla

Mix dry ingredients. Add soft or melted butter, buttermilk, vanilla and eggs. Last, adding water. Bake in preheated oven at 325°-350° till cake is done. Serves 15.

Chocolate Cream Cheese Cake

JOSEPH & RHODA MILLER

1 chocolate cake mix
8 oz. cream cheese
1 egg
½ c. sugar

Mix cake as directed. Cream together cream cheese, egg and sugar. Drop by Tbsp. on cake then marbleize. Bake in a 10"x15" pan at 350° for 25-30 minutes.

187

Topping:
1 box instant vanilla pudding
1 c. milk
8 oz. cream cheese

⅛ c. powdered sugar
3 c. Cool Whip

Cakes & Frostings

Eggless Chocolate Cake

ED & MARY SLABAUGH

3 c. flour
2 c. sugar
1 tsp. salt
6 Tbsp. cocoa
2 c. sour milk
2 tsp. soda
1 tsp. vanilla
½ c. lard, melted

Put all dry ingredients in bowl, except the soda. Dissolve it in the milk. Mix all together, adding melted lard last. Put in a 9"x13" pan. Bake at 350° until done.

Earthquake Cake

JAY & AMY TROYER

1 yellow cake mix
1 c. coconut
1 c. chocolate chips
1 c. nuts
½ c. butter
8 oz. cream cheese
4 c. powdered sugar

Mix cake mix according to instructions on box. Put coconut, chocolate chips and nuts into a 9"x13" pan. Pour cake mix batter over these ingredients. Swirl in cream cheese, butter and powdered sugar (beaten together). Bake at 350° for 1 hour.

188

Earthquake Cake

JACOB & LORETTA WEAVER

3 c. flour
1½ c. sugar
½ c. baking cocoa
2 tsp. soda
1 tsp. salt
1 c. vegetable oil
2 c. water
2 tsp. vinegar
2 tsp. vanilla
1 c. chopped pecans
1 c. shredded coconut

Filling:
½ c. butter or margarine, melted
8 oz. cream cheese, softened
3½ c. powdered sugar

Grease a 9"x13" pan. Sprinkle coconut and pecans on bottom of pan. Measure dry ingredients into bowl and mix, add vegetable oil, water, vinegar and vanilla, mix again. Pour batter over pecans and coconut. Beat cream cheese, powdered sugar and butter. Drop cheese mixture onto cake batter by teaspoon until filling is all used up. Bake at 350° until cake is done (check with toothpick), approx. 50 minutes. Filling will sink into cake resulting in a "hilly" look. But it is very good and best warm!

Option: substitute 1 chocolate cake mix for the batter recipe

189

Gooey Chocolate Cake

MARY LENGACHER

3 c. flour
2 c. sugar
2 tsp. soda
4 Tbsp. cocoa
pinch of salt
¾ c. shortening
1 egg
2 c. sour milk
1 tsp. vanilla

Combine dry ingredients; add shortening and mix to crumbs. Then add egg, milk and vanilla. Beat well. Put in greased 9"x13" pan. Bake at 350° for 30-40 minutes.

Note: A good recipe for beginners, making from scratch.

Cakes & Frostings

Chocolate Chiffon Cake

JOSEPH & RHODA MILLER

7 eggs
1¾ c. sugar
1½ c. Gold Medal flour
¼ c. cocoa
¾ c. hot water
1½ tsp. soda
1 tsp. salt
1 tsp. vanilla
1 tsp. cream of tartar
½ c. vegetable oil

Separate eggs; mix yolks, ¾ c. sugar, vegetable oil, cocoa, soda, salt, vanilla, hot water and flour. Beat whites; add 1 c. sugar and cream of tartar. Gently mix yolk mixture and whites together. Bake in an angel food cake pan at 325° for 15 minutes, then at 350° for 45 minutes.

Swiss Roll Cake

JAY & AMY TROYER, MATTHIAS & NAOMI MAST

1 cooled chocolate cake
8 oz. cream cheese
¾ c. sugar
1 c. marshmallow creme
8 oz. Cool Whip

Topping:
½ c. butter
2 c. chocolate chips

Mix together cream cheese, sugar, marshmallow creme and Cool Whip. Spread on cooled chocolate cake. *Topping:* Melt butter, turn off burner before adding chocolate chips. Drizzle over top of cake. Cut cake before chocolate hardens.

190

Swiss Roll Cake

MARCUS & ROSANNA MAST

1 chocolate cake mix
¾ c. flour
½ c. sugar
1 tsp. baking powder
¼ c. water
1 Tbsp. vegetable oil
1 egg

Mix cake as directed on box, then add rest of ingredients. Pour into an 11"x17" pan. Bake at 325° till done. *White Icing:* Mix together and put on cooled cake. *Chocolate Icing:* Melt butter and chocolate chips and drizzle over white layer.

White Icing:
8 oz. cream cheese
¾ c. sugar

1 c. marshmallow creme
8 oz. Cool Whip

Chocolate Icing:
½ c. butter, melted

2 c. chocolate chips

A Very Good Chocolate Cake

LUKE & KATHRYN MILLER

191

½ c. vegetable oil
1 c. sugar
1 c. brown sugar
2 eggs
¾ tsp. salt
1 c. boiling water
1 c. milk
½ c. cocoa
2 tsp. soda
2 tsp. baking powder
2 c. flour

Beat together oil, eggs, sugars and salt. Mix boiling water and cocoa. Add to mixture. Add soda, baking powder, flour and milk. Mix well. Batter will be thin. Bake at 350° in a 10"x15" or 9"x13" pan until it tests done with a toothpick.

Chocolate Marble Cheesecake

ENOS & NANCY TROYER

Crust:
1 pkg. chocolate cake mix
½ c. Crisco oil or Puritan oil

Filling:
3 (8 oz.) pkg. cream cheese, softened
¾ c. sugar
½ tsp. almond extract
3 eggs
1 sq. (1 oz.) unsweetened
   chocolate, melted

Preheat oven to 350°. Grease a 9" springform pan. *Crust:* Combine cake mix and ½ c. oil in large bowl. Stir until well blended. Press mixture into bottom of pan. Bake at 350° for 22 minutes. Remove from oven. Raise temperature to 450°. *Filling:* Combine first 4 ingredients in large bowl, blend, adding eggs one at a time. Blend mixture after each egg is added. Remove 1 c. filling, add chocolate to filling. Spoon plain filling on warm crust, drop spoonfuls of chocolate filling over plain filling. Swirl with knife. Bake at 450° for 7 minutes. Reduce to 250°. Bake for 30 minutes. Loosen cake edge from pan. Cool before removing from pan. Chill to serve. Serves 12 to 16.

192

Bundt Chocolate Surprise Cake

MARCUS & ROSANNA MAST

8 oz. cream cheese, softened
¼ c. sugar
1 egg
1 tsp. vanilla

Batter:
1 chocolate cake mix
3 oz. instant pudding
4 eggs
1 c. water
½ c. vegetable oil
1 c. chocolate chips

Beat first 4 ingredients together and set aside. Mix batter ingredients together and pour batter into prepared Bundt pan. Evenly cover with cream cheese mixture. Bake at 350° for 45-55 minutes. Cool on wire rack 30 minutes. Remove from pan; cool completely. Drizzle with powdered sugar or icing.

Georgia Peanut Butter Fudge Cake

JOSIAH & RHODA MILLER

1 c. butter
1 c. buttermilk
4 Tbsp. cocoa
½ tsp. salt
1 tsp. soda
2 c. flour
2 c. sugar
1 c. boiling water
2 eggs
1 tsp. vanilla

Icing:
½ c. butter
6 Tbsp. buttermilk
4 Tbsp. cocoa
4 c. powdered sugar
1 tsp. vanilla

Combine first 3 ingredients and bring to a boil. Remove from heat and set aside. Mix dry ingredients in a mixing bowl. Add chocolate mixture to dry ingredients, mix well. Add boiling water, eggs and vanilla, mix well. Pour into a greased 10"x15" jelly roll pan and bake at 350° for 20-25 minutes. Cool cake. Heat 2 c. crunchy peanut butter and spread on cooled cake. *Icing:* Heat first 3 ingredients; add powdered sugar and vanilla. Spread icing over top. Rich, but good!

193

Honey Bun Cake

JUSTIN & NAOMI MILLER

1 yellow cake mix
¾ c. vegetable oil
4 eggs
1 tsp. vanilla
8 oz. sour cream

Mix together and put in jelly roll pan. Sprinkle with topping and swirl. Put glaze on while still hot. Bake at 325° for 40-45 minutes.

Topping:
1 c. brown sugar

1 Tbsp. cinnamon

Glaze:
2 c. powdered sugar
4 Tbsp. milk

1 tsp. vanilla

Angel Food Cake

LARRY & NAOMI LENGACHER

194

1¼ c. flour
¾ c. sugar
1½ c. egg whites
½ tsp. salt
1 tsp. cream of tartar
1 tsp. vanilla
½ tsp. almond flavoring

Beat egg whites to stiff peaks. Mix flour, sugar, cream of tartar and salt in another bowl. Then fold in whites and add vanilla and flavoring. Bake at 375° for 10 minutes, then at 325°-350° until done. Turn upside down on plate till cool.

Orange Zucchini Cupcakes

LUKE & KATHRYN MILLER

6 eggs
2⅔ c. sugar
1 c. vegetable oil
1 c. orange juice concentrate
2 tsp. almond extract
4 tsp. baking powder
2 tsp. soda
2 tsp. salt
5 c. flour
3 c. finely shredded zucchini, packed

Beat together eggs, sugar, oil, orange juice, almond extract, baking powder, soda and salt. Add flour and mix well. Stir in zucchini. Fill cupcake papers ¾ full. Bake at 350° until they test done with toothpick. Ice with white icing after cooling. Yield: 3 doz. These have a soft fluffy texture.

Note: Do not dilute orange juice concentrate.

Super Frosted Cupcakes

STEVIE & REBECCA SWAREY

1 c. flour
1 tsp. baking powder
¼ tsp. salt
6 Tbsp. butter, softened
½ c. sugar
1 lg. egg
⅓ c. milk
½ tsp. vanilla

Frosting:
¾ c. chocolate chips
3 Tbsp. butter
¼ c. + 2 Tbsp. sour cream
¾ tsp. vanilla
⅛ tsp. salt
2 c. powdered sugar

Beat butter and sugar together till light and fluffy. Add egg; mix well. Add remaining ingredients and mix well. Spoon into 24 mini or 12 lg. cupcake pans. Bake at 325° for 12-15 minutes. Cool. Frost.

Note: My 8- and 5-year-old really like to make these for their tea parties. We usually do the minis.

195

Topping for Cake

MATTHIAS & NAOMI MAST

1st Layer:
8 oz. cream cheese, softened
½ c. brown sugar
½ c. powdered sugar
2 c. Cool Whip

2nd Layer:
1 c. sour cream
¼ c. butter
½ c. brown sugar

1st Layer: Have cream cheese at room temperature and beat all together and put on cooled cake. *2nd Layer:* Melt butter; add sugar; melt, then add sour cream. Cook together for 3 minutes. Cool 10 minutes and put on top of cooled 1st layer.

Creamy White Frosting

ATLEE & MATTIE MILLER

¾ c. Crisco
½ tsp. salt
¼ tsp. vanilla
2 Tbsp. water
1 egg white
2 c. powdered sugar (as needed)
1 Tbsp. marshmallow topping

Whip together till fluffy. Put between cookies or use as frosting for cake.

196

Fluffy White Frosting

MATTHIAS & NAOMI MAST

1½ c. Karo
2 egg whites
⅛ tsp. salt
1 tsp. vanilla

Combine egg whites, salt and vanilla. Beat till stiff. Heat Karo to boiling, slowly pour into egg white mixture, beating constantly. Continue beating till frosting is fluffy and stands in peaks.

Brown Sugar Frosting

LEAH TROYER

¾ c. brown sugar
⅓ c. butter
¼ c. evaporated milk
powdered sugar
2 tsp. vanilla

Melt butter, add brown sugar and milk. Bring to a rolling boil and boil for 1 minute. Cool. Add vanilla and powdered sugar to desired consistency. Delicious!

Chocolate Frosting

JAY & AMY TROYER

½ c. butter, softened
⅔ c. cocoa
3 c. powdered sugar
⅓ c. milk
1 tsp. vanilla
cream cheese or Cool Whip
   (optional)

Mix together and spread on top of cooled cake. Very good on yellow cake mix.

197

Chocolate Frosting

JACOB & LORETTA WEAVER

½ c. butter, softened
½ c. Hershey's baking cocoa
3 c. powdered sugar
⅓ c. milk or more
1 tsp. vanilla

Mix well. Add milk or powdered sugar as needed.

Chocolate Frosting

ED & MARY SLABAUGH

1 c. sugar
4 tsp. cocoa
2 Tbsp. cornstarch, heaping
1 c. boiling water
1 tsp. vanilla
2 Tbsp. butter

Mix dry ingredients in saucepan. Pour in the boiling water and cook over medium heat until thickened. Remove from heat, add vanilla and butter. When butter is melted and mixed in, spread on cake. Will have a glossy finish if put on before it's cold.

Chocolate Joy Frosting

JUSTIN & NAOMI MILLER

2⅔ c. powdered sugar
⅓ tsp. salt
3 Tbsp. cocoa
1 lg. egg yolk
⅓ c. soft shortening
5 Tbsp. hot water

Mix hot water and shortening till dissolved. Add cocoa, salt and egg yolk. Mix well. Add powdered sugar till right consistency. For vanilla frosting, eliminate cocoa.

198

Cookies and Bars

Cake Mix Cookies

JOSEPH & RHODA MILLER

1½ c. brown sugar
½ c. sugar
1½ c. butter
6 eggs
2 tsp. soda
5 c. flour
⅛ tsp. salt
½ c. instant chocolate pudding
½ c. instant vanilla pudding
1 chocolate cake mix
1 yellow cake mix

Mix 2 separate batches of first 7 ingredients. Mix chocolate pudding with chocolate cake mix and add 1 batch of dough. Add vanilla pudding to yellow cake mix and add other batch of dough. Let set 30 minutes. Form into small balls, flatten with bottom of glass. Bake at 400° for 8 minutes. Do not overbake! Fill with desired filling. Yield: Approx. 9 doz.

Oreo Cookies

JOSIAH & SUSAN MILLER

2 chocolate cake mixes
1 c. vegetable oil
4 eggs

Filling:
8 oz. cream cheese
¼ c. butter

2½ c. powdered sugar

Mix together until well blended. 1 batch filling is enough for 3 batches cookies. Enjoy!

200

Whoopie Pies

JUSTIN & NAOMI MILLER

1½ c. shortening
3 c. sugar
3 eggs
3 tsp. vanilla
1½ c. cocoa
6 c. flour
3 tsp. soda
3 tsp. salt
1½ c. hot water
1½ c. sour milk

Cream shortening and sugar. Add well beaten eggs, sour milk, vanilla, flour, cocoa and salt. Dissolve soda in hot water. Add to mixture. Bake on greased cookie sheet at 400° for 6-8 minutes. Freezes well.

Filling:
6 egg whites
6 tsp. vanilla
12 Tbsp. milk

12 c. powdered sugar
3 c. Crisco

Oatmeal Whoopie Pies (Little Debbies)

JACOB AND LORETTA WEAVER

201

6 c. brown sugar
2¼ c. margarine
6 eggs
1½ tsp. salt
6½ c. flour
6 c. oatmeal
3 tsp. cinnamon
3 tsp. baking powder
6 tsp. soda
9 Tbsp. boiling water

Cream together sugar and margarine; add eggs, beat well. Add salt, flour, oatmeal, cinnamon and baking powder. Dissolve soda in water and add last. Bake at 325° for approx. 10 minutes. Cool and fill with filling.

Filling:
⅓ c. flour
¾ c. cold water
1 Tbsp. vanilla

1 (2 lb.) bag powdered sugar
1 ½ c. Crisco
½ tsp. salt

Whoopie Pies

IVAN & BARBARA SCHLABACH

4 c. sugar
2 c. shortening
4 eggs
4 egg yolks
2 tsp. salt
5½ tsp. soda
2 c. cocoa
2½ c. boiling water
8 c. flour
2 c. sour milk

Filling:
4 egg whites, beaten
4 tsp. vanilla
½ c. flour
3 Tbsp. milk

2 c. Crisco
8 c. powdered sugar
marshmallow creme

Combine first 5 ingredients; mix well. Add next 3 ingredients; mix well. Add flour and sour milk. Chill dough. Bake at 400°. Cool and fill. *Filling:* Cream first 5 ingredients. Add powdered sugar a little at a time, then add marshmallow creme.

Oatmeal Creme Pies

202

MATTHIAS & NAOMI MAST

2¾ c. butter
2½ c. brown sugar
2 c. cane sugar
6 eggs, blended with
   3 c. raisins or dried cranberries
6 c. oatmeal
1 Tbsp. soda
1 Tbsp. baking powder
1 Tbsp. cinnamon
1 Tbsp. vanilla
½ Tbsp. salt
5 Tbsp. water
6 c. flour

Filling:
4 egg whites, beaten stiff
2 tsp. vanilla
1 c. butter
4 c. powdered sugar

Cream together butter and sugars; add blended eggs and raisins. Blend in remaining ingredients. Bake at 350° till golden. Fill with Whip-n-Ice or filling.

Debbie Cookies

JOSIAH & SUSAN MILLER

1 c. butter
1½ c. brown sugar
1½ c. sugar
4 eggs
1 tsp. salt
1½ tsp. soda
2 tsp. cinnamon
½ tsp. nutmeg
2 tsp. vanilla
3 c. flour
3 c. oatmeal

Cream together butter and sugar; add eggs and blend very well. Add rest of ingredients and bake at 350°. Do not bake cookies too long or chill overnight. Our favorite filling is Whip-n-Ice, which we buy at our local bulk food store.

Filling:
2 egg whites, beaten
1 tsp. vanilla

3 c. powdered sugar
1 c. butter

Delicious Debbies

MATTHIAS & NAOMI MAST

203

4 c. brown sugar
2¼ c. butter
6 c. oatmeal
6 eggs
3 tsp. vanilla
3½ c. flour
2¼ tsp. soda
3 tsp. cinnamon
1½ tsp. salt

Mix together sugar and butter. Add eggs and mix well. Add vanilla and dry ingredients. Mix. Bake at 350° till golden. Will be soft and chewy if not overbaked. *For Filling:* Mix all together and beat well.

Filling:
4 egg whites, beaten
2 tsp. vanilla

4 c. powdered sugar
1 c. butter

Caramel Press Cookies

VERNON & RUTH YODER

1 c. butter
¾ c. brown sugar
¾ c. sugar
2 eggs
2 tsp. vanilla
3½ c. flour
1 tsp. salt
½ tsp. soda

Mix all ingredients together. Put through press, can also drop. Bake at 350°. Melt together butter, milk and marshmallows, then add vanilla and powdered sugar. A double batch of everything makes 2½ doz. cookies.

Filling:
4 Tbsp. butter
2 Tbsp. milk
6 lg. marshmallows

1 tsp. vanilla
2 c. powdered sugar or more

Chocolate Sandwich Cookies

STEVE & MIRIAM LENGACHER

204

4¾ c. margarine
7 c. sugar
8 eggs
8 tsp. vanilla
8 c. flour, maybe more
2 c. cocoa
4 tsp. soda
1 tsp. salt

Cream margarine and sugar. Then add eggs, vanilla, salt, soda and cocoa, and last add flour. Don't bake too hard. Bake at 350°.

Filling:
1 egg, beaten
1 tsp. vanilla
5 Tbsp. milk

½ c. Crisco, scant
powdered sugar

Oatmeal Raisin Cookies

JACOB & LORETTA WEAVER

1½ c. sugar
1½ c. brown sugar
1¾ c. shortening or butter
2 tsp. vanilla
4 eggs
1 tsp. salt
2 tsp. soda
1 tsp. baking powder
3 c. flour
5 c. oatmeal
raisins, as desired

Mix sugars and shortening; add eggs and vanilla. Last add dry ingredients and raisins. Roll into balls and bake at 300°-325° until set. Do not brown! Very good and soft.

Oatmeal Sandwich Cookies

MICHAEL & JOANNE COBLENTZ

1½ c. shortening
2⅔ c. brown sugar
4 eggs
2 tsp. vanilla
2¼ c. flour
1 tsp. cinnamon
1½ tsp. soda
4 c. oatmeal
1 c. chocolate chips

Cream shortening and sugar. Add eggs and mix well. Add rest of ingredients in order given. Bake at 350°.

205

Filling:
¾ c. shortening
3 c. powdered sugar

7 oz. marshmallow creme
1-3 Tbsp. milk

Oatmeal Chocolate Chip Cookies

MARCUS & ROSANNA MAST

1½ c. butter
2 c. sugar
2 c. brown sugar
4 eggs
2 tsp. vanilla
6 c. quick oats
4 c. all-purpose flour
2 tsp. soda
1 tsp. salt
2 c. chocolate chips

In a bowl cream butter, sugars, eggs and vanilla. Combine oats, flour, soda and salt. Stir into a creamed mixture, then add chocolate chips; mix well. Drop cookies on greased cookie sheet. Bake at 325° for 12-13 minutes or until lightly browned. Yield: 7 doz.

All-Purpose Oatmeal Chocolate Chip Cookies

STEVIE & REBECCA SWAREY

1½ c. flour
1 tsp. soda
½ tsp. salt
1½ tsp. cinnamon
1 c. butter, softened
½ c. brown sugar
1 c. sugar
1 egg
1 tsp. vanilla
1½ c. oatmeal (old fashioned)
1 c. chocolate chips

Beat together butter and sugar till light and fluffy. Beat in egg and vanilla. Stir in dry ingredients until well blended, fold in chocolate chips.

Options on this recipe: Omit chocolate chips and fill with filling and they are very good Debbie Cookies or omit chocolate chips and put in raisins for Raisin Oatmeal.

206

Classic Chocolate Chip Cookies

ENOS & NANCY TROYER

3 c. butter
¾ c. sugar
2¼ c. brown sugar
3 tsp. vanilla
1½ c. instant vanilla pudding
6 eggs
6¾ c. flour
3 tsp. soda
3 c. chocolate chips or more
almond slices or walnuts (optional)
M & Ms

Mix butter, sugars and eggs; add instant vanilla pudding and vanilla flavoring, then flour and soda and last nuts, chocolate chips and M&M's. Yield: Approx. 16 doz.

Chocolate Chip Cookies

STEVE & MIRIAM LENGACHER

2 c. margarine or butter
2 c. brown sugar
1 c. sugar
4 eggs
2 tsp. vanilla
½ tsp. salt
2 tsp. soda
5 c. flour
2 c. chocolate chips

Cream shortening and sugars. Beat in eggs and vanilla. Add flour, soda and salt. Stir just until blended. Fold in chocolate chips. Bake at 350° for 10-12 minutes. Yield: 5 to 6 doz.

207

Cookies & Bars

Chocolate Chip Cookies

JOSHUA ERIC WEAVER

2 c. sugar or evaporated
   cane sugar
2 c. brown sugar or Sucanat
1½ c. butter, softened
4 eggs
1 tsp. baking powder
2 tsp. soda
1 tsp. salt
2 tsp. vanilla
4 c. whole wheat flour
4 c. oatmeal
2 c. chocolate chips
2 c. walnuts

Cream together sugar and butter. Blend in eggs. Add the rest of the ingredients, mixing well. Bake on ungreased cookie sheet for 8-10 minutes at 400°. These cookies are better if they are slightly under baked, rather than overbaked. Yield: 4 doz.

Chocolate Chip Cookies

LARRY & NAOMI LENGACHER

4½ c. flour
1 c. oatmeal
2 tsp. soda
2 c. margarine
½ c. sugar
1½ c. brown sugar
2 tsp. vanilla
2 pkg. chocolate chips
1 c. nuts (optional)
4 eggs
2 pkg. vanilla instant pudding

Mix sugars and margarine, then add pudding, eggs, vanilla, soda, oatmeal, flour and chocolate chips. Bake at 350° until lightly brown.

208

Just Right Chocolate Chip Cookies

JOSIAH & SUSAN MILLER

2 c. butter
1½ c. sugar
1½ c. brown sugar
5 eggs
1 tsp. vanilla
1 tsp. water
2 tsp. salt
2 tsp. soda
½ c. instant vanilla pudding
1 c. chocolate chips
6 c. flour

Mix butter and sugar until creamy. Add eggs and beat until fluffy. Add rest of ingredients and bake at 350°.

Note: Better if not baked too hard.

Chocolate Chip Cookies

MARY LENGACHER

1 c. shortening
1½ c. margarine
1½ c. brown sugar
1½ c. sugar
4 eggs
4 tsp. vanilla
1⅓ c. instant vanilla pudding
2 tsp. salt
2 tsp. soda
6 c. flour
3 c. chocolate chips

Cream shortening, margarine and sugars. Mix in eggs. Add vanilla and pudding, then rest of dry ingredients. Add chocolate chips last. Bake at 350° for 8-10 minutes. Yield: Approx. 6 doz.

Our favorite.

209

Cookies & Bars

Chocolate No-Bake Cookies

MATTHIAS & NAOMI MAST

4 c. sugar
1 c. milk
⅔ c. cocoa
1 c. butter
8 c. quick oats
1 c. peanut butter
2 tsp. vanilla

Mix first 4 ingredients in large saucepan and bring to a boil. Boil 1 minute. Remove from heat and add quick oats, peanut butter and vanilla. Mix well, then drop by spoonful on wax paper and let set till firm.

Monster Cookies

STEVE & MIRIAM LENGACHER

2 c. brown sugar
2 c. sugar
1 c. margarine
3 c. peanut butter
6 eggs
9 c. quick oats
1½ tsp. corn syrup
1½ tsp. vanilla
4 tsp. soda
½ tsp. salt
2-3 c. M&M's
2-3 c. chocolate chips

Mix in order given. Bake at 350°. Do not overbake.

210

Monster Batch Monster Cookies

MATTHIAS & NAOMI MAST

1½ c. butter
2 c. cane sugar
2 c. Sucanat
8 eggs
2 lb. peanut butter
5 tsp. soda
9 c. oatmeal
1 lb. mini M&M's (optional)
3 c. chocolate chips

Cream butter and sugars; add eggs, peanut butter and soda. Blend in oatmeal and chocolate chips.

Molasses Cookies

JOSIAH & RHODA MILLER

1½ c. vegetable oil
1½ c. sugar
2 eggs
½ c. molasses
4 tsp. soda
1 Tbsp. ginger
1 tsp. salt
2 tsp. cinnamon
4 c. flour

Mix together and chill for 2 hours or overnight. Roll in balls and white sugar. Bake at 325° for 10 minutes.

211

Molasses Cookies

JOSIAH & SUSAN MILLER

1½ c. shortening
3½ c. sugar
¼ c. molasses or sorghum
4 eggs
3 tsp. soda
1 tsp. baking powder
½ tsp. ground cloves
2 tsp. cinnamon
1 tsp. salt
7 c. flour

Cream together shortening and sugar; add eggs and beat very well. Add rest of ingredients and bake at 350°.

Filling:
1 c. Crisco
2 tsp. vanilla

4 c. powdered sugar
2 egg whites

Molasses Crinkle Cookies

JUSTIN & NAOMI MILLER

¾ c. margarine
1 c. brown sugar
¼ c. molasses
1 egg
2¼ c. flour
1 tsp. ginger
1 tsp. cinnamon
¼ tsp. salt
2 tsp. soda
½ tsp. cloves

Mix all ingredients. Bake at 350° for 8 minutes. Yield: 3½ doz.

Soft Molasses Cookies

ENOS & NANCY TROYER

5 c. shortening
(can use half butter)
5 c. sugar
6 eggs
1½ c. molasses
3 tsp. salt
4 tsp. cinnamon
12 tsp. ginger
12 tsp. soda
15 c. flour

Bake at 350° for 12-15 minutes.

Molasses Cookies

MARY LENGACHER

½ c. butter or margarine
½ c. shortening
1½ c. sugar
½ c. baking molasses
2 eggs
4 c. flour
½ tsp. salt
2¼ tsp. soda
1½ tsp. ginger
1½ tsp. cloves
1½ tsp. cinnamon

Mix butter, shortening and sugar; add molasses, then eggs; mix well. Add dry ingredients. Let set in bowl in refrigerator a couple hours or overnight. Shape in small balls and roll in sugar. Bake at 350° for 9-10 minutes. Yield: 3½-4 doz. cookies.

213

Cookies & Bars

Grandma's Sugar Cookies

LARRY & NAOMI LENGACHER

3 c. sugar
3 c. brown sugar
3 c. lard
6 eggs
4½ c. milk
3 tsp. soda
9 tsp. baking powder
6-8 c. flour
1 tsp. vanilla
1 tsp. maple flavoring
1 tsp. lemon flavoring
1 tsp. salt

Mix sugars and lard well; add eggs, milk, soda, baking powder, flavorings and flour. Roll out on flat surface, cut with cutters. Frost with favorite frosting. Bake at 425° for 8-10 minutes.

Sugar Cut-Out Cookies

JOSIAH & RHODA MILLER

214

1 c. butter
1½ c. powdered sugar
1 egg
½ tsp. almond extract
1 tsp. vanilla
1 tsp. baking soda
1 tsp. cream of tartar
2½ c. flour

In mixing bowl, cream butter and sugar. Add egg and mix well. Add rest of ingredients. Chill dough for a couple of hours. Roll out on floured surface and cut with cookie cutters. Bake at 375° for 7-8 minutes. Cool and frost.

White Icing:
4 c. powdered sugar
¾ c. Crisco
¼ c. milk
1 tsp. white vanilla

¼ tsp. almond flavoring
1 tsp. butter flavoring
pinch of salt
¼ c. Karo

Raisin Puffs

MATTHEW & MARLENE TROYER, MATTHIAS & NAOMI MAST

2 c. water
4 c. raisins
3 c. sugar
2 c. butter
4 eggs
2 tsp. vanilla
7 c. flour
2 tsp. soda
½ tsp. salt

Cook water and raisins till water is almost gone. Cool. Mix butter, sugar and eggs. Add rest of ingredients and mix well. Then add raisins. Roll each cookie in white sugar before putting on sheets to bake. Bake at 350°.

Frosted Ginger Cookies

JOSIAH & RHODA MILLER

1½ c. butter
¾ c. sugar
1 c. brown sugar
2 eggs
½ c. molasses
2 tsp. vanilla
4½ c. flour
1 Tbsp. ginger
2 tsp. soda
2 tsp. cinnamon
½ tsp. salt
½ tsp. cloves

Frosting:
½ c. butter
3 c. powdered sugar
4 Tbsp. boiling water
1½ tsp. vanilla

In a mixing bowl, cream butter and sugars. Add eggs; beat well. Stir in molasses and vanilla; mix well. Add soda, salt and spices, mixing well. Stir in flour. Drop onto ungreased cookie sheet. Bake at 350° for 12-14 minutes. *Frosting:* Melt butter in saucepan; cook over medium heat, stirring constantly, until butter stops bubbling and is nut brown in color. (Do not scorch.) Combine with powdered sugar and boiling water; beat until smooth and of spreading consistency. Add vanilla, and add more hot water if it gets too thick.

215

Dipped Gingersnaps

ELAINA FAITH YODER (AGE 4)

2 c. sugar
1 c. butter
4 tsp. soda
2 eggs, beaten
½ c. molasses
1 tsp. ginger
2 tsp. salt
4 c. flour

Cream sugar and butter. Add eggs, molasses and dry ingredients. Bake at 350° for 10-12 minutes. Dip half of cooled cookie in white coating.

Gingersnaps

JAMES & IDA LEHMAN

3 c. shortening
4 c. brown sugar
4 eggs
1 c. molasses
9 c. flour
8 tsp. soda
4 tsp. cinnamon
4 tsp. ginger
2 tsp. cloves
2 tsp. salt

Mix first 4 ingredients. Add all the rest of the ingredients. Roll into balls and dip in white sugar. Place on baking sheet. Bake at 350° for 10-12 minutes. Yield: Approx. 5 doz.

216

Peanut Butter Jumbos

MICHAEL & JOANNE COBLENTZ

1½ c. peanut butter
½ c. butter, softened
1 c. sugar
1 c. brown sugar
3 eggs
1 tsp. vanilla
4 c. oatmeal
2 tsp. soda
½ c. chocolate chips
1 c. M&M's

Mix together and drop on ungreased cookie sheets. Bake at 350° for 10 minutes or until slightly brown. Do not overbake.

Pumpkin Chip Cookies

LARRY & NAOMI LENGACHER

1½ c. butter
2 c. brown sugar, packed
1 c. sugar
1 (15 oz.) can pumpkin
1 egg
1 tsp. vanilla
4 c. flour
2 c. oatmeal
2 tsp. soda
2 tsp. cinnamon
1 tsp. salt
2 c. chocolate chips

In a large mixing bowl, cream butter and sugars. Add pumpkin, egg and vanilla. Combine the flour, oats, soda, cinnamon and salt; add to creamed mixture. Last add chocolate chips. Bake at 350° for 10-12 minutes. Yield: 10 doz.

217

Cookies & Bars

Strawberry Creme Cookies

JACOB & LORETTA WEAVER

1 c. butter, softened
1 c. sugar
3 oz. cream cheese, softened
1 Tbsp. vanilla
1 egg yolk
2½ c. flour
strawberry jam

Mix butter, sugar and cream cheese; add vanilla and egg yolk. Blend in flour. Chill dough. Roll into 1" balls. Use a floured thimble (or similar choice) to poke a hole in the center. Fill with jam. Bake at 325°-350° on ungreased pan. Remove from oven as soon as edges begin to brown and center looks done. Best served warm.

Soft Date Cookies

MICHAEL & JOANNE COBLENTZ

218

2 c. chopped dates
¾ c. water
½ c. sugar
2 c. brown sugar
1 c. shortening
3 eggs
1 tsp. soda in 1 Tbsp. water
1 tsp. salt
1 tsp. vanilla
3½-4 c. flour

Boil dates, water and sugar over low heat for 5 minutes. Cool. Mix rest of ingredients together except flour, then add date mixture. Add flour. Bake at 350°. Do not overbake. When cool, roll in powdered sugar.

Twinkies

VERNON & RUTH YODER

1 yellow cake mix
1 box instant vanilla pudding
4 eggs
¾ c. vegetable oil
¾ c. water

Filling:
3 egg whites
3 c. powdered sugar
1 c. Crisco
marshmallow creme (optional)
1 tsp. vanilla

Mix cake mix, instant vanilla pudding, eggs, oil and water. Line jelly-roll pan with wax paper. Put ½ of batter in pan. Bake at 350°. Remove cake with wax paper. Bake rest of cake. *For Filling:* Mix egg whites, powdered sugar, Crisco, marshmallow creme and vanilla. Spread filling between 2 layers. Enjoy!

Peanut Butter Swirl Bars

LARRY & NAOMI LENGACHER, MARY LENGACHER

⅓ c. butter
½ c. peanut butter
¾ c. sugar
¾ c. brown sugar
2 eggs
1 tsp. vanilla
1 c. flour
1 tsp. baking powder
¼ tsp. salt
12 oz. (1½ c.) chocolate chips

Cream butter, peanut butter and sugars together. Add eggs, mix well. Stir in flour, salt, baking powder and vanilla. Put in greased 9"x13" pan. Top with chocolate chips. Bake 5 minutes. Remove from oven and run knife through batter to make swirls of chocolate chips. Bake another 15 minutes at 350°.

219

Cookies & Bars

Chocolate Streusel Bars

JACOB & LORETTA WEAVER

1¾ c. flour
1½ c. powdered sugar
½ c. baking cocoa
1 c. margarine
8 oz. cream cheese
14 oz. can sweetened
  condensed milk
1 egg
2 tsp. vanilla
½ c. nuts, chopped

Combine flour, sugar and cocoa, cut in margarine until crumbly. Mixture will be dry. Reserve 2 c. crumb mixture, press remainder in bottom of a 9"x13" pan. Bake at 350° for 15 minutes. Beat cream cheese until fluffy, beat in sweetened condensed milk until smooth, add egg and vanilla. Mix well. Pour over crust. Mix nuts with reserved crumbs, spread on top. Bake at 350° for 25 minutes or till bubbly. Cool, chill and cut.

Marbled Chocolate Bars

LARRY & NAOMI LENGACHER

1 chocolate cake mix
8 oz. cream cheese, softened
½ c. sugar
¾ c. chocolate chips

Prepare cake batter according to package. Pour into a greased 15"x10"x1" pan. In a small bowl beat cream cheese, sugar and ¼ c. chips. Drop by Tbsp. over batter. Cut through with knife, sprinkle with rest of chocolate chips. Bake at 350° for 25 minutes. Yield: 3 doz.

220

Lemon Cream Cheese Bars

MATTHEW & MARLENE TROYER

1 lemon cake mix
⅓ c. vegetable oil, scant
2 eggs
8 oz. cream cheese
1 c. sugar
1½ c. lemon drops

Combine cake mix, oil and 1 egg together until crumbly. Reserve 1 c. for top. Pat remaining crumbs in a 9"x13" pan. Beat cream cheese, sugar and 1 egg. Spread over cake mixture. Sprinkle with reserved crumbs and lemon drops. Bake at 325° for approx. 30 minutes. Do not overbake.

Butterscotch Zucchini Bars

LUKE & KATHRYN MILLER

3 eggs
⅔ c. vegetable oil
2 c. sugar
2 tsp. vanilla
2½ c. flour
2 tsp. soda
1 tsp. salt
½ tsp. baking powder
2 c. finely shredded zucchini,
   packed

Beat together eggs, sugar, oil and vanilla. Beat in soda, salt and baking powder. Mix in flour till well mixed. Stir in zucchini. Pour into greased 15"x10"x1" pan. Mix together topping and sprinkle over batter in pan. Bake at 350° for 30 minutes or until it tests done with a toothpick. Also good with a thin glaze drizzled over the top.

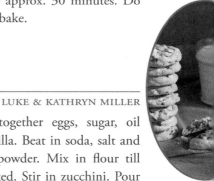

221

Topping:
½ c. brown sugar
1 c. butterscotch chips

Cookies & Bars

Sour Cream Chocolate Chip Squares

MATTHIAS & NAOMI MAST

1 c. butter
1 c. brown sugar
1¾-2 c. flour
1¾-2 c. quick oats
1 tsp. baking powder
1 tsp. soda
1 tsp. salt

Filling:
4 egg yolks
1½ c. chocolate chips
1 c. sugar
2 Tbsp. clear jel
2 c. sour cream

Cream together butter and brown sugar. Add rest of ingredients. Set aside 2 c. of mixture. Press remaining crumbs into greased 11"x17" pan. Bake at 350° for 15 minutes. Cool. Combine filling ingredients in a saucepan, except chocolate chips. Bring to a boil, stirring, and boil for 5 minutes. Pour over crust. Sprinkle with chocolate chips. Sprinkle with remaining crumbs. Return to oven for 15 minutes.

O' Henry Bars

MATTHIAS & NAOMI MAST

4½ c. quick oats
1 c. brown sugar
½ tsp. salt
1 c. butter
½ c. light corn syrup
1¾ c. chocolate chips
½ c. peanut butter
1 tsp. vanilla

Mix first 3 ingredients well; add butter and corn syrup and mix well again. Press into a 9"x13" pan. Bake at 350° for 20 minutes or till edges start to bubble. Cool slightly. Melt chocolate chips and peanut butter. Remove from heat and add vanilla. Spread over oatmeal mixture. Cool before cutting and refrigerate.

Yum-Yum Bars

LARRY & NAOMI LENGACHER

2 c. sugar
¾ c. margarine
1 c. flour
½ tsp. salt
4 eggs
1 tsp. vanilla
½ c. cocoa
½ c. nuts (optional)

Cream margarine and sugar well; add eggs, vanilla and dry ingredients. Bake at 350° for 25 minutes. Put into a 9"x13" pan. Sprinkle powdered sugar on top when done.

Gooey Chocolate Bars

STEVIE & REBECCA SWAREY

1¾ c. flour
¾ c. powdered sugar
¼ c. cocoa
1 c. margarine

Filling:
1 c. chocolate chips
1 (14 oz.) can condensed milk
1 tsp. vanilla

Mix first 4 ingredients and press into a 9"x13" pan. Bake for 15 minutes. *For Filling:* Melt together ingredients. Pour over crust, sprinkle with nuts and bake another 15 minutes. (I use the homemade sweetened condensed milk recipe found in this cookbook.)

223

Friendship Fruit Bars

JOHN & ESTA YODER

1 c. butter, softened
2 c. brown sugar
3 c. flour
1 tsp. salt
1 tsp. soda
3 c. oatmeal
6 Tbsp. water
2 pt. canned fruit pie filling
   of your choice

Cream butter and sugar. Add flour, salt, soda and water. Add oatmeal last. Put ½ of mixture into greased cookie sheet. Sprinkle with pie filling and crumble the rest of mixture on top. Bake at 350° for 25-30 minutes.

Chocolate Chip Cream Cheese Bars

JOSIAH & SUSAN MILLER

1 yellow or chocolate cake mix
⅓ c. vegetable oil
⅓ c. sugar
2 eggs
8 oz. cream cheese
1 c. milk chocolate chips

Mix cake mix, 1 egg and oil until crumbly. Reserve 1 c. for topping. Put remaining mixture into 9"x13" pan. Bake at 350° for 15 minutes. Beat cream cheese, sugar and 1 egg until light and smooth, stir in chocolate chips, and spread over baked layer. Sprinkle with remaining crumbs. Bake for 15 minutes.

224

Cream Cheese Bars

STEVE & MIRIAM LENGACHER

1 yellow or chocolate cake mix
1 egg, beaten
⅓ c. vegetable oil
8 oz. cream cheese, softened
1 c. chocolate chips
1 egg
1 can Eagle Brand milk

Mix dry cake mix, egg and oil until crumbly. Reserve 1 c. for topping. Pat remaining crumbs into greased cake pan. Bake at 350° for 10-12 minutes. Beat cream cheese, Eagle Brand milk and egg until fluffy. Spread on baked layer. Sprinkle with chocolate chips and reserved crumbs. Return to oven and bake 10 minutes. Serves 24.

Cream Cheese Bars

IVAN & BARBARA SCHLABACH

2 (8 oz.) cream cheese
2 c. sugar
1½ tsp. vanilla
4 cans crescent rolls
½ c. sugar
1 tsp. cinnamon
2 Tbsp. butter, melted

Roll out 2 cans crescent rolls into a 10"x15" pan. Beat first 3 ingredients together. Spread on top. Roll out 2 cans crescent rolls and put on top. Mix last 3 ingredients together. Sprinkle on top. Bake at 350° for 30 minutes.

225

Cowboy Bars

MATTHIAS & NAOMI MAST

1 c. butter
1 c. sugar
1 c. brown sugar
2 eggs
1½ tsp. vanilla
¼ c. milk
1½ tsp. soda
½ tsp. salt
2 c. quick oats
1½ c. chocolate chips
¾ c. nuts (optional)
1 c. coconut
2 c. flour

Cream together butter and sugar and add remaining ingredients. Spread evenly in 11"x17" pan. Bake at 350° for 20-30 minutes. Do not overbake. When still slightly warm, drizzle with icing.

Apple Bars

ED & MARY SLABAUGH

1 c. flour
½ tsp. soda
½ tsp. salt
½ c. brown sugar
1 c. quick oats
½ c. shortening
¼ c. brown sugar
2½ c. sliced apples

Combine the first 6 ingredients, making crumbs. Spread half of crumbs in a 9"x9" pan. Place apples on crumbs, sprinkle with ¼ c. brown sugar and cover with remaining crumbs. Bake at 350° for 40-50 minutes.

226

Clark Bars

ENOS & NANCY TROYER

1 box graham crackers, crushed
18 oz. creamy peanut butter
2½ c. powdered sugar
1 c. butter, melted
1 can Eagle Brand milk
12 oz. chocolate chips

Mix crushed graham crackers, peanut butter, powdered sugar and melted butter. Press into a 10"x16" pan. Combine sweetened condensed milk with chocolate chips. Melt in double-boiler. Pour over top and refrigerate.

Granola Bars

STEVIE & REBECCA SWAREY

¾ c. brown sugar
⅔ c. peanut butter
¼ c. corn syrup or honey
½ c. butter
2 tsp. vanilla
3 c. oatmeal
½ c. coconut
⅓ c. whole wheat flour
⅓ c. wheat germ (optional)
1 c. raisins
½ c. chocolate chips

Mix first 5 ingredients well. Blend together and add the rest of the ingredients. Press into a 9"x13" pan. Bake at 350° for 10-15 minutes or till lightly brown. Do not overbake. You may substitute 2 c. of church peanut butter for the first 3 ingredients. A good way to use that leftover peanut butter.

227

Granola Bars

MATTHIAS & NAOMI MAST

2 (10 oz.) pkg. marshmallows
¾ c. butter
¼ c. peanut butter (optional)
5 c. oatmeal
4½ c. Rice Krispies
1 c. coconut
1 pkg. graham crackers (optional)
chocolate chips (optional)

Melt butter and peanut butter; stir in marshmallows. Heat only till melted. Add remaining ingredients, stir well and press into a 10"x15" pan. For a good variation you can melt 1½ c. chocolate chips and ¼ c. peanut butter and spread on top.

Granola Bars

MICHAEL & JOANNE COBLENTZ

3 c. oatmeal
4½ c. Rice Krispies
1 c. coconut
2 pkg. graham crackers, crushed
1 c. mini M&M's
½ c. mini chocolate chips
¾ c. butter
¼ c. peanut butter
¼ c. honey
¼ c. vegetable oil
1½ lb. mini marshmallows

In a 6 qt. kettle melt butter, peanut butter, honey and oil. Add marshmallows and stir until melted. Mix dry ingredients together and add to kettle. Mix together and press into a well buttered 11"x17" cookie sheet. Cool and cut.

228

Granola Bars

MARCUS & ROSANNA MAST

2 c. brown sugar
½ c. sugar
1½ c. butter
8 c. oatmeal
3 c. milk chocolate chips
3 c. peanut butter

Mix sugars, butter and oatmeal until crumbly. Press into an 11"x17" cookie sheet and bake at 330° for 20 minutes. Melt chocolate chips and peanut butter. Spread on top of first mixture.

Granola Bars

AARON THOMAS WEAVER

½ c. butter
4 c. sm. marshmallows
5-5½ c. granola
mini chocolate chips

Melt butter in large saucepan. Add marshmallows and stir. (Turn off heat before they're completely melted. This keeps them softer.) Add granola and stir. Spread in greased 9"x9" pan. Sprinkle chocolate chips over top and press down. Do this quickly so they'll melt and stick. (Do not put in while stirring, they'll melt completely!) Cool and cut. These are good and chewy. Children really like them! Recipe times 2 makes large sheet.

229

Texas Brownies

ENOS & NANCY TROYER

2 c. all-purpose flour
2 c. sugar
½ c. butter
½ c. Crisco shortening
1 c. strong brewed coffee
¼ c. baking cocoa
½ c. buttermilk
2 eggs
1 tsp. soda
1 tsp. vanilla

Frosting:
½ c. butter
2 Tbsp. dark cocoa
¼ c. milk
3½ c. powdered sugar
1 tsp. vanilla

In large mixing bowl, combine flour and sugar. In heavy saucepan, combine shortening, butter, coffee and baking cocoa. Stir and heat to boiling. Pour over flour/sugar mixture; add eggs, buttermilk, soda and vanilla. Mix well. Bake at 400° for 20 minutes on 17½"x11" (well greased) pan. While brownies bake, heat butter, cocoa and milk to boiling, stirring. Remove from heat and add powdered sugar and vanilla. Pour warm frosting over brownies as soon as you take them out of oven. Cool, cut in 48 bars.

230

Sue's Brownies

MATTHIAS & NAOMI MAST

1½ c. butter
2½ c. sugar
6 eggs
¾ c. cocoa
¾ tsp. baking powder
¾ tsp. salt
3 tsp. vanilla
3 c. flour

Cream butter and sugar; add eggs and remaining ingredients. Spread evenly in 11"x17" pan. While still warm sprinkle with powdered sugar. For variation sprinkle with chocolate chips before baking. Bake at 350° for 35 minutes.

Canning and
Freezing

Rhubarb Slush Drink

MATTHIAS & NAOMI MAST

12 qt. rhubarb
2½ c. sugar
2 c. water
2 Tbsp. strawberry or raspberry
  Jell-O
2 c. pineapple juice
½ c. ReaLemon

Cut up rhubarb into 1"-2" chunks. Put in large kettle and cover with water. Boil for 10 minutes. Pour into colander and strain, saving juice. Melt sugar and water. Add remaining ingredients, pour into strained rhubarb juice. Put into freezer containers and freeze. Thaw slightly and add a 2-liter warm Sprite or 7-Up. Serve while still slushy.

Blueberry-Rhubarb Freezer Jam

STEVIE & REBECCA SWAREY

5 c. fresh or frozen rhubarb
½ c. water
5 c. sugar
1 (21 oz.) can blueberry pie
  filling
2 c. fresh or frozen blueberries
3 Tbsp. lemon juice
2 (3 oz.) pkg. raspberry Jell-O

In a large kettle, cook rhubarb and water over medium heat for 5 minutes or till rhubarb is tender. Add sugar, bring to a boil, and boil for 2 minutes. Stir in pie filling, blueberries and lemon juice. Return to a boil, reduce heat, cook and stir for 10 minutes. Remove from heat. Stir in Jell-O till dissolved, cool slightly. Pour into containers, cool to room temperature. Cover and refrigerate or freeze. We really like this jam. Also, I just make my own blueberry pie filling. Yield: 4½ pts.

232

Rhubarb Preserves

ED & MARY SLABAUGH

8 c. chopped rhubarb
6 c. sugar
6 oz. Jell-O

Simmer together for 15 minutes. Take off heat and add the Jell-O. When dissolved put in jars and seal.

Strawberry Jam

MATTHEW & MARLENE TROYER, JUSTIN & NAOMI MILLER

4 c. strawberries
4 c. sugar
⅓ c. + 2 Tbsp. instant clear jel

Mix sugar and instant clear jel well before adding to strawberries. Add to berries and stir for 10 minutes. Yield: 3 pts.

Apple Pie Filling

MATTHIAS & NAOMI MAST

3 c. sugar
1 c. brown sugar
1½ c. clear jel
1 tsp. cinnamon
1 tsp. apple pie spice
2 Tbsp. butter
3 Tbsp. lemon juice
1 tsp. salt
10 c. water
14 c. chopped apples

Heat water, sugar and clear jel, stirring constantly, until thickened. Add spices, lemon juice and butter. Mix well and add apples. Put in jars. Hot water bath for 20 minutes.

233

Apple Pie Filling

MATTHEW & MARLENE TROYER

9 c. brown sugar
6 c. sugar
7 c. Therm-Flo
½ c. lemon juice
3 Tbsp. cinnamon, rounded
¾ c. butter
1 Tbsp. salt
at least ½ bu. apples (15 qt. shredded)
12 qt. water
2 qt. water to mix with Therm-Flo

Mix and heat 12 qt. water with sugar, juice, cinnamon, butter and salt. Bring to boil and add Therm-Flo which has been added to 2 qt. of water. Bring to boil and add apples. Fill jars and cold pack for 20 minutes. Yield: 25 qt.

Peach Pie Filling

MATTHIAS & NAOMI MAST

16 c. water
6 c. sugar
3½ c. Fridgex
½ c. Karo
3 (3 oz.) pkg. peach Jell-O
1 (3 oz.) pkg. pineapple Jell-O
2 Tbsp. lemon juice

Mix first 3 ingredients and boil until thick and clear. Stir in rest of ingredients and cool. Add peaches to suit your taste.

234

Peach Pie Filling

JUSTIN & NAOMI MILLER

9 c. pineapple juice
7 c. water, divided
8 c. sugar
½ c. Karo
¾ c. peach Jell-O
½ c. pineapple Jell-O
½ c. orange Jell-O
3 c. Therm-Flo
10 qt. peaches
½ c. lemon juice

Cook juice, 3 c. water, sugars, Jell-Os together till boiling. Mix 3 c. Therm-Flo and 4 c. water. Pour into hot mixture, very slowly, stirring constantly till thick. Remove from heat; add ½ c. lemon juice and fruit. Put in jars and cold pack for 10-15 minutes. More fruit can be used. I like to open a jar and add other fruit, such as grapes, pineapple, apples and have mixed different fruits. Very refreshing. Yield: Approx. 12 qt.

Red Raspberry Pie Filling

MATTHIAS & NAOMI MAST

1½ qt. water
1½ qt. raspberry pureé
4 c. Fridgex
6 c. sugar
½ c. black raspberry Jell-O
1 tsp. salt
1 Tbsp. lemon juice
2 tsp. vanilla

Heat first 4 ingredients till thickened, then add rest of ingredients.

Blueberry Pie Filling

JOHN & ESTA YODER

10 c. water
5 c. sugar
3 Tbsp. ReaLemon juice
1 c. pineapple juice

Mix ingredients together and heat. Thicken with 2½ c. Perma Flo. Add ½ c. black raspberry Jell-O and ½ c. blueberry Jell-O. Then add 5 qt. blueberries or less. Cold pack 10 minutes. Yield: 8 qt.

Blueberry Pie Filling

MATTHEW & MARLENE TROYER

27 c. water
12 c. sugar
12 c. blueberries
5¼ c. Therm-Flo
blueberry Jell-O

Cook first 3 ingredients for 5 minutes, then add Therm-Flo which has been mixed with water. Cook until thickened. Add blueberry Jell-O to suit your taste. Stir in blueberries to desired consistency. Put in jars and cold pack for 10 minutes. Yield: Approx. 15 qt.

236

Blueberry Pie Filling

JOSIAH & RHODA MILLER, JUSTIN & NAOMI MILLER

5 qt. water, divided
9-9½ c. sugar
4 c. mashed blueberries
2¾ c. Therm-Flo
4 tsp. vanilla
2 tsp. salt
2½ Tbsp. lemon juice
fresh blueberries

Combine 4 qt. water, sugar and mashed blueberries in large kettle. Bring to a boil; cook a few minutes. Add Therm-Flo (which had been mixed with 1 qt. water) to the blueberry mixture and bring to a boil, cooking for at least 1 minute. Remove from heat and add rest of ingredients. Put in jars and cold pack for 10-15 minutes. Yield: Approx. 10 qt.

Black Cherries

MATTHEW & MARLENE TROYER

3 c. black raspberry Jell-O
4 c. sugar
14 c. boiling water
11 qt. washed & stemmed
cherries

Mix first 3 ingredients, stir till Jell-O and sugar are dissolved. Pour over cherries which have been put into jars. Hot water bath for 10 minutes.

Peach Pineapple Slush

JOSIAH & RHODA MILLER

5 (12 oz.) cans frozen orange juice
30 oz. frozen lemonade
10 c. sugar
15 c. water
5 qt. fresh peaches, sliced
3 fresh pineapples, cut & cubed
40 bananas, sliced or chunked
red grapes, couple bunches

Dissolve sugar in warm water. Add orange juice and lemonade. Mix in fruit and stir well. Yield: Approx. 20 qt.

237

Fruit Slush

MICHAEL & JOANNE COBLENTZ

7 c. sugar
10 c. boiling water
4 (12 oz.) cans orange juice
1 lg. can pineapple juice
2 lt. 7-Up
6 qt. sliced peaches
2 whole pineapples, cut up
grapes
20 bananas

In 20 qt. canner mix sugar and water. Add rest of ingredients. Put in freezer containers and freeze.

Tapioca to Can

MATTHIAS & NAOMI MAST

8½ qt. water
6 c. pearl tapioca
¼ tsp. salt
7 c. Jell-O
6 c. sugar

Bring water to a boil, then add tapioca and salt. Boil for 5 minutes, let set for 30 minutes, then add Jell-O and sugar. Hot water bath for 30 minutes.

Canning Pumpkins or Butternut Squash

MATTHIAS & NAOMI MAST

pumpkins or squash
¾-1 c. water
1 tsp. salt
1 tsp. pumpkin pie spice

Cut up pumpkins or squash, remove seeds, put in large kettle and cook with a little water. Cook until soft. Cool and peel pumpkins. Place peeled pumpkin in blender and add rest of ingredients. Pour into jars and hot water bath for 1½ hours.

238

Green Beans

MATTHIAS & NAOMI MAST

To 1 qt. beans add:
1 tsp. salt
1 tsp. lemon juice
1 c. water

Process for 2 hours.

Zucchini Relish

MATTHIAS & NAOMI MAST

1 gal. ground zucchini
1 pt. ground onions
1 red, orange & yellow
    pepper (optional)
¼ c. salt
2 tsp. mustard seed
2 tsp. celery seed
2 tsp. turmeric
4 c. sugar
2 c. vinegar

Add salt to first 3 ingredients and let set for 2 hours. Drain for 4-5 hours. Mix rest of ingredients and bring to a boil; pour over drained zucchini mixture. Ladle into jars and hot water bath for 10 minutes.

Garlic Dills

MATTHIAS & NAOMI MAST

cucumbers, sliced
3 c. cane sugar
1 c. vinegar
3 c. water
2 Tbsp. salt
garlic
dill

Mix sugar, vinegar, water and salt and heat. In a qt. jar put 2 garlic cloves or ¼ tsp. minced garlic and 1 dill head or 1 tsp. dill seed. I prefer them with fresh dill if available. Fill jars with sliced cucumbers. Pour in hot syrup. Top with hot lids and rings and set in oven on pan at 265° for 25 minutes. Remove and turn upside down. Ready to eat in 2 weeks. A quick way to can a lot of pickles at once.

239

Jalapeño Peppers

IVAN & BARBARA SCHLABACH

turmeric
alum
1 qt. vinegar
1 c. salt

Wash and slice peppers. Pack into jars. Add ⅛ tsp. turmeric and ⅛ tsp. alum to each jar. Put salt and vinegar into a gallon pitcher. Fill with water, then bring to boil. Pour into jars and seal.

Frozen Hot Peppers

MATTHIAS & NAOMI MAST, STEVIE & REBECCA SWAREY

1 peck hot peppers
   (jalapeño or banana)
⅛ c. oregano
1 whole garlic
2½ c. vegetable oil
½ c. salt
1 qt. vinegar
1 qt. water

Cut peppers in strips or rings. Add rest of ingredients. Let set a few hours or overnight, stirring occasionally. Put in glass jars or freezer containers and freeze. Using plastic containers will make your freezer smell like peppers.

240

Mustard Peppers

JOSIAH & SUSAN MILLER

1 qt. water
3 qt. vinegar
1 c. brown sugar
1 c. salt
1 c. mustard
½ tsp. alum

Can use for banana or hot peppers. Heat until almost boiling. Put in jars, heat lids, then seal in oven at 265° for 30 minutes.

Hot Pepper Butter

SAMUEL & LEANNA WEAVER

40 hot peppers, ground
2 c. mustard
1 qt. vinegar
6 c. sugar
1 Tbsp. salt
1 c. flour
1½ c. water

Bring to a boil. Add flour mixed with water, boil 5 minutes. Seal in jars.

Barbecue Peppers

JOHN & ESTA YODER

32 oz. pizza sauce
1 Tbsp. salt
6 oz. ketchup
1 c. vinegar
2 c. sugar
¼ c. vegetable oil

Boil this for 10 minutes; add 1 gal. pepper rings, cut up. Cook for 1-3 minutes. Add to jars while hot and seal. Do not cold pack. You can use sweet peppers, banana peppers and onions to make 1 gal. Yield: 7-9 pt.

241

Canning Peppers

MATTHIAS & NAOMI MAST

1 qt. water
3 qt. vinegar
1 c. brown sugar
1 c. salt
½ c. mustard
½ tsp. alum
garlic cloves

Cut peppers into thin strips or rings and pack into jars. Put 1 slice garlic clove in each jar. Combine all ingredients in saucepan. Heat to almost boiling; pour over peppers in jars. Cover with hot lids and rings. Put in oven at 265° for 25 minutes. Remove and turn jars upside down.

Italian Peppers

IVAN & BARBARA SCHLABACH

1 bottle Italian dressing
1 qt. vinegar
1 pt. vegetable oil
¾ c. water
½ c. salt
⅓ c. oregano
2 cloves garlic

Combine all ingredients. Slice banana peppers and add to brine. Set out at room temperature for 24 hours, then refrigerate or freeze.

Pepper Mustard

JOSIAH & SUSAN MILLER

36-40 banana or hot peppers
1 qt. mustard
1 qt. vinegar
1 Tbsp. salt
6 c. sugar

Put peppers through Salsa Master or blender. Boil together, then thicken with 1½ c. flour and ¾ c. water. Use some of the vinegar to mix with flour, as ¾ c. water is not enough. Cold pack for 10 minutes. Yield: Approx. 10 pt.

242

Jalapeño Pepper Butter

MATTHIAS & NAOMI MAST

15 banana peppers
10 green peppers
10 jalapeño peppers
3 c. mustard
4 c. vinegar
5 c. cane sugar
1 Tbsp. salt
1½ c. flour
2 c. water

Chop peppers in food processor; add remaining ingredients, except for flour and water. Make a paste with flour and water and stir into boiling pepper butter. Ladle into jars and hot water bath for 10 minutes.

Ketchup

JOHN & ESTA YODER

16 qt. chopped tomatoes
6 onions, chopped

Cook tomatoes and onions. Put through a sieve or use blender. Drain in a jelly bag overnight or half a day. Discard the juice. Bring the pulp that's in the bag to a boil, then add 1 c. vinegar, 1 c. water (or use less water if it's going to be too runny) 4 c. evaporated cane juice, 3 Tbsp. salt and 1 Tbsp. ketchup spice. Cook 10 minutes and seal. Begin timing after ketchup comes to a rolling boil. Yield: 5-6 pt.

Marinara Sauce

MATTHEW & MARLENE TROYER

13 qt. tomato juice, cooked
    with 4 lg. onions
1 gal. tomato paste
6-8 c. Sucanat
2½ tsp. oregano
4 tsp. garlic salt
3 minced garlic cloves
3 Tbsp. dry mustard
1 qt. ketchup
3 Tbsp. garlic powder
3 Tbsp. chili powder
5 Tbsp. parsley
2 green peppers, cut up

Boil for 30 minutes. Mix 3 pkg. Mrs. Wages pizza sauce with around 2 c. Therm-Flo and enough water to mix. Bring to boil again to thicken after Therm-Flo mixture is added. Next add 16 oz. Parmesan cheese and mix well. Put in jars. Hot water bath pts. for 20 minutes and qts. for 30 minutes. You need to cold pack these a little longer, with the cheese. Yield: Approx. 16-17 qt.

243

Pizza Sauce

JOSEPH & RHODA MILLER

2½ gal. tomato juice
8 med. onions
4 green peppers
1 pt. vegetable oil
2 Tbsp. basil
1½ c. brown sugar
2 Tbsp. oregano
½ Tbsp. red pepper
½ c. salt
1 Tbsp. Italian seasoning
1 tsp. garlic powder
3 Tbsp. pizza seasoning
1 gal. tomato paste

Simmer 1 hour. Cold pack 45 minutes. Yield: 15-17 qt.

Barbecue Sauce

MATTHIAS & NAOMI MAST

244

15 c. tomato juice
4 c. chopped onions
¾ c. ReaLemon
5 c. Sucanat
⅔ c. cane sugar
3 c. vinegar
¾ c. mustard
⅔ c. Liquid Smoke
⅔ c. salt
2 c. Worcestershire sauce
⅓ c. paprika
½ Tbsp. garlic salt
1 c. honey
1 c. molasses

Bring to a boil. Make a paste with 2 c. cornstarch and 3 c. cold water or tomato juice. Slowly add to hot mixture, stirring quickly with a wire whisk to blend. Bring back to a boil, stirring constantly. Ladle into jars. Hot water bath for 20 minutes.

Barbecue Sauce

MICHAEL & JOANNE COBLENTZ

4 qt. tomato juice
3 sm. onions
2 c. sugar
¾ c. vinegar
2 Tbsp. salt
½ tsp. pepper
1 Tbsp. pickling spice
1 tsp. dry mustard
1 c. Therm-Flo
3 c. brown sugar
2 Tbsp. mustard
2 Tbsp. Liquid Smoke
½ Tbsp. garlic salt
60 oz. ketchup
1 bottle honey mustard
    barbecue sauce
1 c. molasses
1 c. honey

Blend tomatoes and onions together, enough to make 4 qt., or put through Victorio strainer. Add sugar, vinegar, salt and pepper. Put pickling spice and mustard in a bag and add. Cook for 1½ hours. Mix Therm-Flo and brown sugar together and slowly add to tomato mixture, stirring well. Add rest of ingredients and mix well. Put in jars and cold pack for 20 minutes.

245

Barbecue Sauce

MARCUS & ROSANNA MAST

4 qt. tomato juice
  (1 peck tomatoes)
3 sm. onions
2 c. sugar
2 tsp. salt
¾ c. vinegar

In a bag put:
1 Tbsp. pickling spice
1 tsp. dry mustard
½ tsp. black pepper

Cook together tomato juice and onions and put through strainer, then add sugar, salt and vinegar. Put pickling spice, dry mustard and black pepper in a bag. Cook 1½ hours with tomato mixture. Remove bag and add rest of ingredients; thicken with 1 c. clear jel and water, bringing to a boil. Cold pack 30 minutes.

1 bottle barbecue sauce
1 c. molasses
1 c. honey
60 oz. ketchup
3 c. brown sugar

½ Tbsp. garlic salt
2 tsp. mustard
Liquid Smoke to taste
Worcestershire sauce to taste

246

Salsa

IVAN & BARBARA SCHLABACH

3 gal. tomatoes
3½ c. onions
5 green peppers
1-2 hot peppers (optional)
½ c. vinegar
⅓ c. sugar
2 Tbsp. salt
1 Tbsp. oregano
1½ Tbsp. chili powder
1½ tsp. cumin
garlic
1 pkg. Mrs. Wages salsa
6-8 Tbsp. Therm-Flo

Blanch and peel tomatoes. Dice tomatoes, onions and peppers. Add remaining ingredients other than Therm-Flo. Simmer till soft. Thicken with Therm-Flo and water. Pour into jars and seal.

Salsa

SAMUEL & LEANNA WEAVER

6 hot peppers with seeds
10 sweet peppers
14 lb. tomatoes
2½ lb. onions
1 c. vinegar
¼ c. sugar
¼ c. salt
1½ Tbsp. garlic powder (or add
   several cloves instead)
2 Tbsp. chili powder
2 Tbsp. oregano
1 c. Therm-Flo (or similar thickener)
liquid hot sauce to taste, if needed

Chop vegetables (first 4 ingredients) fine or put through Salsa Master. Cook in a large kettle till tender, about 10 minutes. Add the spicy gravy mixture and bring to a boil. Ladle into jars and cold pack 10 minutes. Yield: 18 pt.

247

Peach Salsa

MATTHEW & MARLENE TROYER

25 med. tomatoes
2 sm. onions, chopped
2 peppers, chopped
1 pkg. Mrs. Wages salsa mix
 (mild)
1½ c. sugar
½ c. vinegar, scant
½ pkg. taco seasoning
½ tsp. oregano
1 tsp. basil
2 tsp. parsley
3 Tbsp. garlic salt, rounded
1-2 pt. peach jam
Therm-Flo

Cut tomatoes up in small pieces. Add rest of ingredients except jam and Therm-Flo. Bring to a boil till vegetables are soft. Mix Therm-Flo with some water and add to mixture, then add jam. Put in pt. jars and put in hot water bath for 20 minutes. Yield: around 16 pt.

Salsa

MATTHIAS & NAOMI MAST

20 qt. tomatoes, chopped
10 c. onions, chopped
10 c. mild hot peppers, chopped
10 c. green peppers, chopped
2½ c. vinegar
1 c. salt
5 Tbsp. chili powder
2½ Tbsp. cumin
5 Tbsp. garlic salt, rounded
2½ c. brown sugar
1 gal. tomato paste

Chop tomatoes and heat, drain off some of liquid. Add onions and peppers. In large bowl combine tomato paste, vinegar, spices and sugar. Add to chopped tomatoes. Fill jars and process 30 minutes.

Thick and Chunky Salsa

JUSTIN & NAOMI MILLER

16 lb. tomatoes, scalded, skinned
and squooshed
10 cloves garlic, sliced
6 sweet peppers, chunked,
as desired
3 Tbsp. oregano
1 Tbsp. garlic salt
3 Tbsp. cumin
¼ c. salt
4 jalapeño peppers, sliced
4 lg. onions
1 c. clear jel
¾ c. sugar
1 c. vinegar

Mix all except clear jel. Boil 15 minutes. Add clear jel (with water). Boil till it thickens. Cold pack 15 minutes. Yield: Approx. 10 qt. Be sure to have a bag of chips handy. Very good.

Vegetable Soup

VERNON & RUTH YODER

249

6-7 qt. tomato juice
½-2 lb. fried hamburger
2 c. cooked spaghetti or alphabets
½ c. sugar
2 Tbsp. chili powder, level
salt to taste
1 qt. diced carrots, raw
1 qt. diced potatoes, raw
1 qt. corn
1 qt. diced celery, raw
1 qt. chopped onions, raw
1-2 cans chili beans

Mix together all ingredients, put in jars and pressure can at 10 lb. pressure for 1½ hours or cold pack 3 hours. Yield: 15-17 qt.

Cream of Tomato Soup

JOSIAH & SUSAN MILLER

16 qt. tomato juice
5 onions
12 lg. peppers
4½ c. flour
3 c. sugar
¾ c. salt
9 tsp. black pepper
1 lb. butter

Put onions and peppers through blender. Melt butter, add onions and peppers, fry a little. Stir in flour, sugar, salt and black pepper. And cook a little. Add tomato juice. Put in blender. Yield: Approx. 21 qt. To serve: Add ⅔ jar of milk to jar of soup.

Frozen Corn

MATTHEW & MARLENE TROYER

12 c. raw corn
1 Tbsp. salt
½ c. sugar
1 c. water

Mix and bring to a boil, stirring often. Cool. Put in bags and freeze.

250

To Can Bologna

MATTHIAS & NAOMI MAST

bologna
1 gal. water
⅓ c. salt
½ c. brown sugar

Fill jars with bologna; dilute tomato juice with ½ water, pour over bologna in jars and process 45 minutes; or for a different flavor, heat water, salt and brown sugar; melt and pour over bologna in jars. Process 45 minutes.

Ham Chunks to Can

JAMES & IDA LEHMAN

1½ c. Tender Quick
2 c. brown sugar
1 Tbsp. black pepper
½ c. Liquid Smoke
6 c. cold water

Mix all together and pour over approx. 20 lb. chunked ham or beef. Soak 6 days in a cool place. If meat chunks are coarsely ground, soak only 3 days. Pressure can quarts 1 hour at 10 lb. Very handy to add to soups or casseroles. Yield: Approx. 10 qt.

Deer Meat –
For Breakfast Sausage Patties

JAMES & IDA LEHMAN

50 lb. deer meat
25 lb. sausage
1¼ c. salt
4 Tbsp. black pepper
4 tsp. dry mustard
½ c. sage
1 c. brown sugar

Mix dry ingredients. Sprinkle over meat and mix well before grinding. Put in family size packages and freeze. A good way to use up some of that deer meat.

251

Chunk Beef to Can

MATTHIAS & NAOMI MAST

16 lb. chunk beef
1 c. brown sugar
1 gal. water
1 c. salt
1 tsp. salt petre
2 tsp. soda

Boil brine, cool and add chunk beef. Soak for 5 days. Drain and rinse. Fill jars with beef.

RECIPE FOR _____

_____
_____
_____
_____
_____
_____
_____
_____
_____
_____
_____
_____
_____
_____

RECIPE FOR _____

_____
_____
_____
_____
_____
_____
_____
_____
_____
_____
_____
_____
_____
_____

Candies, Snacks and Miscellaneous

Cream Cheese Mints

JENNIFER MILLER

4 oz. cream cheese
12 drops flavoring
3 c. powdered sugar
food coloring

Divide cream cheese into 3 bowls (1¼ oz. to each one). Divide rest of ingredients to bowls. Mix well and spread on wax paper or put in candy molds. Let set in refrigerator for 1 hour. Cut in small squares. Roll in white sugar and let dry.

Mini Cheesecakes

REBEKAH MAST (AGE 11)

12 vanilla wafers
2 (8 oz.) pkg. cream cheese
½ c. sugar
1 tsp. vanilla
2 eggs

Place 1 vanilla wafer in each cupcake liner. Mix cream cheese, vanilla and sugar until well blended. Add eggs, mix well. Pour on top of wafer, ¾ full. Bake at 325° for 25 minutes. Cool and top with fruit. Serves 12.

254

Mini Pizzas

JOSEPH & RHODA MILLER

1 tube biscuits
pepperoni
cheese
pizza sauce

Flatten biscuits and spread pizza sauce on top. Then top with pepperoni and cheese. Bake at 375° for 10-15 minutes or until golden brown. Serves 6.

Marshmallow Hats

RACHEL MAST (AGE 9)

12 Ritz crackers
12 lg. marshmallows
peanut butter

Spread each cracker with peanut butter. Put 1 marshmallow on each cracker. Put in 350° oven till marshmallows are soft.

Easter Nests

STEVE & MIRIAM LENGACHER

7 oz. jar marshmallow creme
¼ c. peanut butter
2 Tbsp. butter, melted
5 oz. chow mein noodles
1 c. pastel M&M's
powdered sugar
½ c. pastel peanut butter M&M's
    or reg. M&M's

Cream marshmallow creme, peanut butter and butter until smooth. Fold in noodles and M&M's. Chill on wax paper. Form mixture by ⅓ c. into 3" nest. Chill 30 minutes. Dust with powdered sugar. Place several peanut butter M&M's in each nest. You can also use jelly beans.

255

Muddy Buddies

JANEVA LANAE & JAPHETH LYNN YODER (AGES-2)

12 c. Rice Chex
½ c. butter
½ c. peanut butter
12 oz. chocolate chips
2½ c. powdered sugar

Put Chex in bowl; melt together butter, peanut butter and chocolate chips. Stir until smooth. Pour over Chex and mix well. Add powdered sugar; stir until well coated. Cool. Store in airtight container. Yummy!

Puppy Chow

RACHEL MAST (AGE 9)

¼ c. butter
1 c. chocolate chips
¾ c. peanut butter
8 c. Crispix
1½-2 c. powdered sugar

Melt together butter, chocolate chips and peanut butter; pour over Crispix; toss and dust with powdered sugar.

Cow Pies

ADRIAN TITUS WEAVER

2 c. chocolate chips
1 Tbsp. butter
½ c. raisins
½ c. chopped, slivered almonds

In a saucepan, melt chocolate chips and butter, stirring till smooth. Remove from heat, stir in raisins and almonds. Drop by Tbsp. onto waxed paper. Chill till ready to serve. Yield: 2 doz. Serves 12.

256

Honey Peanut Butter Balls

LARRY & NAOMI LENGACHER

½ c. corn syrup or honey
½ c. peanut butter
½ c. Rice Krispies
¾ c. Mike powder

Mix together corn syrup or honey and peanut butter. Add Rice Krispies and Mike powder. Roll in balls. Roll balls in wheat germ or coconut.

A good snack after school.

Crisp-Rice Roll-Ups

JON DANIEL YODER (AGE 6)

5½ c. Crisp Rice cereal
1 pkg. sm. marshmallows
¼ c. butter

Filling:
1¼ c. chocolate chips
¼ c. peanut butter

Melt butter and marshmallows; add cereal; stir well. Spread cereal mixture on buttered surface. *Filling:* Melt chocolate chips; add peanut butter. Spread filling over cereal mixture and roll up. Cut after chilled.

Peanut Butter Cups

MARCUS & ROSANNA MAST

1 c. powdered sugar
1 c. peanut butter
¼ c. butter, softened
⅛ tsp. salt

Mix together and chill well. Form into balls. Put in mini cupcake candy liners. Cover with melted chocolate. Chill. Delicious!

Date Balls

257

MARY LENGACHER

½ c. margarine
¾ c. sugar
1 (8 oz.) box dates, chopped
1 c. nuts (optional)
2 c. Rice Krispies

Blend margarine, sugar and dates in heavy saucepan. Boil until thick (watch carefully). Remove from heat and add nuts and Rice Krispies. When cool to touch, squeeze into balls and roll in powdered sugar or press into greased 8"x8" pan for bars and sprinkle with powdered sugar. Cut when cooled completely.

Cayenne Pretzels

MARY SUANN TROYER

1 c. vegetable oil
1 pkg. dry ranch dressing mix
1 tsp. garlic powder
1 tsp. cayenne pepper
2 pkg. (10 oz. pkg. each) pretzels

Bake at 200° for 1½-2 hours.

Ranch Pretzels

KRYSTAL DAWN MILLER

½ c. butter
1 pkg. ranch dressing mix
1 c. brown sugar
1 lb. pretzels

Mix sugar and ranch mix. Melt butter and pour over pretzels. Pour sugar mixture over buttered pretzels. Very easy.

Sweet-N-Salty Pretzels

LUKE & KATHRYN MILLER

1 lb. pretzels
¾ c. vegetable oil or butter, scant
1 pkg. ranch dip mix
1 c. brown sugar

Pour butter over pretzels. Mix till coated. Add ranch dip mix and brown sugar. Toss till coated. Bake at 310° for 1 hour.

Cheddar-Ranch Pretzels

IVAN & BARBARA SCHLABACH

1 lb. pretzels
¾ c. vegetable oil
3 Tbsp. cheddar powder
3 Tbsp. ranch dip mix

Stir together oil, cheddar and ranch mix. Toss pretzels till evenly coated. Bake at 250° for 30 minutes.

Spiced Pretzels

LARRY & NAOMI LENGACHER

¼ tsp. garlic salt
½ tsp. lemon pepper
½ tsp. dill weed
3 Tbsp. ranch dressing or
   sour cream powder, rounded
1 c. vegetable oil
24 oz. pretzels

Mix spices with vegetable oil; pour on pretzels; let set on counter, stirring often, until oil is all absorbed. Yield: 2 ice cream pails.

Heavenly Hash

MARY LENGACHER

5 c. Honey Nut Cheerios
5 c. Captain Crunch peanut
   butter
3 c. mini marshmallows
3 c. Spanish peanuts
2 lb. white chocolate coating

Mix cereal, marshmallows and peanuts together. Melt white chocolate and pour over mixture. Place by spoonfuls on greased trays. Makes a big batch.

259

Sweet Party Mix

MATTHIAS & NAOMI MAST

1 lb. butter
1 lb. honey
1 lb. brown sugar
1 lb. Honey Combs
1 lb. Rice Chex
1 lb. Corn Chex
1 lb. pretzels
1 lb. M&M's

Mix together last 5 ingredients. Melt butter, honey, and sugar together and pour over first mixture. Bake at 325° for 20 minutes.

Delicious Party Mix

JAY & AMY TROYER

1½ c. margarine
4 Tbsp. Worcestershire sauce
1 c. vegetable oil
4 tsp. paprika
4 tsp. celery salt
4 tsp. onion salt
1 box Cheerios
1 box Corn Chex
1 pkg. pretzel sticks
1 can stick potato chips
M&M's

Melt together first 6 ingredients; pour over mix and stir.

Party Mix

CHERYL ANNE YODER

1 box Corn Chex
1 box Rice Chex
1 box Honey Combs
1 box Cheerios
1 bag waffle pretzels
1 box chocolate chip cookie cereal
M&M's
3 c. butter
1 Tbsp. Lawry's seasoned salt
2 Tbsp. Worcestershire sauce
1 tsp. celery salt
½ tsp. onion salt
1 tsp. salt

Mix cereal together. Melt butter; add rest of ingredients. Stir into cereal. Bake in roaster pans at 250° for 1½ hours, stirring every 15 minutes. Add M&M's when cooled.

Party Mix

JULIA GRACE YODER (AGE 10)

1 lg. box Honey Combs cereal
1 lg. box Crispix or any Chex
   cereal
1 lg. box Cookie Crisp cereal
1 bag Bugles
1 bag mini pretzels or
   pretzel sticks
1 bag corn chips
cashews or any nuts of your
   choice
½ c. butter
½ c. vegetable oil
½ tsp. onion salt
½ tsp. garlic salt
½ tsp. celery salt
1 Tbsp. seasoning salt
3-4 Tbsp. Worcestershire sauce

Mix together cereals and cashews. Stir together sauce ingredients and heat. Pour over snack, mix well and bake at 250° for approx. 1 hour. Stir every 15 minutes. Cool.

261

Pigs in a Blanket

MARY LENGACHER

1 pkg. lil smokies sausages
2 (8 oz.) cans crescent rolls

Cut each crescent roll in half lengthwise. Wrap it around a sausage. Place on cookie sheet, apart from each other. Bake at 375° for 10-12 minutes or till golden brown. Yield: 32 little "piggies."

A favorite for children.

Caramel Popcorn

JOSHUA ERIC WEAVER

1 c. butter
1½ c. Sucanat
½ c. honey
½ tsp. soda
1 tsp. vanilla
¼ tsp. cream of tartar

Bring butter and sweeteners to a boil in saucepan, boil 4 minutes or less, stirring constantly. Remove from heat. Add remaining ingredients and pour over 5-7 qt. popped corn. Stir till coated. Bake on cookie sheet at 225° for 1 hour. Stir every 10-20 minutes while baking and cooling. Enjoy your snack! Serves 8.

Crisp Caramel Corn

JUSTIN & NAOMI MILLER

7 qt. popcorn
2 c. brown sugar
½ c. light Karo
¾ c. margarine
½ tsp. soda
1 tsp. vanilla

Boil first 4 ingredients for 5 minutes. Remove from heat and add soda and vanilla. Bake at 350° for 1 hour, stirring every 15 minutes. Very crisp!

262

Cinnamon Popcorn

REBEKAH MAST (AGE 11)

¾ c. lg. popcorn
½-¾ c. cinnamon imperials
¼ tsp. salt
4 Tbsp. vegetable oil

Heat oil; add popcorn, cinnamon imperials and salt. Pop and enjoy.

Taco Seasoning Mix

JOSIAH & SUSAN MILLER

6 Tbsp. chili powder
2 Tbsp. garlic powder
4 Tbsp. onion powder
2 Tbsp. paprika
2 Tbsp. oregano
1 Tbsp. salt

Combine all ingredients and blend well. 3 Tbsp. mix equals 1¼ oz. pkg. store-bought.

Homemade Velveeta Cheese

STEVIE & REBECCA SWAREY

1 gal. milk
2 tsp. citric acid
¼ c. butter
2-3 Tbsp. cheddar cheese powder
1 tsp. salt
1 tsp. soda
¼ c. cream or milk

Heat milk to 140° (no hotter). Remove from burner immediately. Sprinkle 2 tsp. citric acid over top of warmed milk, let set 1 minute. Stir gently till it is separated, add ½ tsp. more of citric acid if it doesn't separate. Drain gently, squeezing it to remove as much whey as possible. Melt ¼ c. butter in kettle, add cheese chunk, cheddar cheese powder, salt and soda. Stir briskly over low heat till all lumps are melted, add cream. If it is too thin, do not add cream. Use as you would Velveeta cheese.

263

Homemade Sweetened Condensed Milk

STEVIE & REBECCA SWAREY

1 c. instant dry milk
⅔ c. sugar
⅓ c. boiling water
3 Tbsp. butter

Mix together, beat until smooth. Use in recipes that ask for 1 can sweetened condensed milk.

Candies, Snacks & Miscellaneous

Fluffy Peanut Butter Spread

MATTHIAS & NAOMI MAST

40 oz. Jif peanut butter
2 lb. 3.2 oz. dessert & pastry
   topping
1½ c. pancake syrup

Thaw dessert and pastry topping and whip; add peanut butter and pancake syrup. Use Jif peanut butter for best results.

Peanut Butter Spread

MATTHEW & MARLENE TROYER

5 lb. peanut butter
2 (35 oz.) dessert & pastry
   topping
24 oz. pancake syrup

Whip both toppings–not too stiff. Beat in with peanut butter and syrup. This will fill a fix-n-mix bowl.

Friendship Brownies (in a quart jar)

JENNIFER MILLER

264

1 c. sugar
1 c. chocolate chips
½ c. chopped walnuts
1 c. brown sugar, not packed
⅔ c. cocoa
½ tsp. baking powder
½ tsp. salt
1 c. flour

Layer in jar in order given. Press down well after each layer. Put directions below on card and attach to jar.

Add to dry mixture:

4 eggs, 1 c. vegetable oil and 2 tsp. vanilla. Put in a 9"x13" greased pan. Bake at 350° for 35-40 minutes. Sprinkle with powdered sugar. Enjoy!

Makes a neat little gift.

Easy Cottage Cheese

LUKE & KATHRYN MILLER

1 gal. milk
½ c. vinegar

Heat milk to boiling or 190°. Take off heat and add vinegar. Let set 10-15 minutes. Drain and rinse. Add cream and salt to taste.

Blackberry Syrup

MATTHIAS & NAOMI MAST

Fill a qt. jar ½ full with blackberries, then fill up with glycerin. Let set for 1 month, strain and use as an immune booster.

Play Dough

KENDRA JOY YODER (AGE 5)

265

3 Tbsp. vegetable oil
4 tsp. cream of tartar
2 c. water
1 c. salt
2 c. flour
food coloring

Mix ingredients together in pan. Cook over medium heat until mixture starts to boil or form a ball (about 2-3 minutes). Remove from heat and cool enough to handle. Knead like bread dough till smooth and supple. Have fun!

Happy Home Recipe

MARY LENGACHER

4 c. love
2 c. loyalty
3 c. forgiveness
1 c. friendship
5 spoons hope
2 spoons tenderness
2 qt. faith
1 barrel laughter

Take love and loyalty, mix it thoroughly with faith. Blend it with tenderness, kindness and understanding. Add friendship and hope. Sprinkle abundantly with laughter. Bake it with sunshine. Serve daily with generous helpings.

A Happy Marriage Recipe

VERNON & RUTH YODER

3 c. love
2 c. warmth
1 c. forgiveness
1 c. friends
4 Tbsp. hope
2 Tbsp. tenderness
1 pt. faith
1 barrel laughter

Combine love and warmth, mix thoroughly with tenderness. Add forgiveness, blend with friends and hope. Sprinkle all remaining tenderness, stir in faith and laughter. Bake with sunshine. Serve in generous heapings.

266

Large Quantity

Apricot Nectar Salad

2 c. boiling water
2 sm. boxes apricot Jell-O
2 c. apricot nectar
½ can crushed pineapple
2 c. grapes (cut in ½)

Dissolve apricot Jell-O in boiling water. When dissolved add apricot nectar. Chill; add pineapple and grapes; pour into bowls. Recipe x26 feeds approx. 550 people.

Bing Cherry Salad

Bottom Layer:
½ c. black cherry Jell-O
1½ c. hot water
1½ c. cold water

Center:
⅓ c. black cherry Jell-O
1 c. hot water
8 oz. cream cheese
3 c. Cool Whip

Bottom Layer: Dissolve Jell-O in water and pour into a 9"x13" pan. *Center Layer:* Dissolve Jell-O in water and let partially set; add cream cheese and Cool Whip. Let set and top with another layer of plain Jell-O. 25 pans feeds approx. 550 people.

268

Layer Salad

ED & MARY SLABAUGH

9 heads lettuce
36 c. shredded cabbage
18 c. shredded carrots
9 c. chopped celery
9 c. chopped green peppers
5 c. finely chopped onions
5 lb. shredded cheese
18 tomatoes, chopped
9 lb. bacon, fried & cut up

Chop up the day before into separate containers. Layer in serving bowls, half full, put on dressing, then repeat layers. Do not add all the vinegar at once—test and taste. Serves about 500.

Dressing:
20 c. salad dressing
10 c. sugar
7 Tbsp. salt

½ c + 2 Tbsp. mustard
2½ c. vinegar
3½ Tbsp. celery salt

Potato Salad for Weddings

MARY LENGACHER

269

60 lb. cooked, diced potatoes
12 doz. hard-boiled eggs
12 med. onions, chopped
6 c. chopped celery
24 c. salad dressing
3 c. mustard or less
3 c. vinegar
6 c. milk
12 c. sugar
½ c. salt

Mix potatoes, eggs, onion and celery together. Mix dressing together and pour over potato mixture. Refrigerate overnight. Serves 400. Yield: 12 gallons.

Homemade Noodles

MATTHIAS & NAOMI MAST

3 doz. egg yolks
1½ c. boiling water
4 lb. Softex flour
1 Tbsp. salt

Put flour in large bowl and weigh out 4 lb. Beat eggs and add boiling water; beat again; add salt. Make sure water is boiling and add quickly. Beat until foamy. The longer you beat, the lighter the noodles. Add flour gradually.

Gravy

1 gal. broth
6 egg yolks
7 Tbsp. flour, rounded
6 Tbsp. cornstarch, rounded
1 Tbsp. chicken base
½ tsp. salt

Put everything in blender, except broth. I blend 1 batch at a time, then pour into hot broth.

Chicken Gravy

LUKE & KATHRYN MILLER

4 qt. chicken broth
2 c. potato water
2 c. clear jel
1 qt. water
4 Tbsp. chicken base
1 tsp. seasoning salt
¼ tsp. pepper

Bring broth and potato water to boil in 6 qt. kettle. In another bowl mix clear jel with 1 qt. water. Stir into broth. Cook until thickened. Add seasonings. Yield: Approx. 6 qt.

Dressing

12 eggs, beaten
¾ ice cream pail deboned
   chicken with 2 qt. broth
1 handful parsley, cut up
2 c. diced carrots
2 c. diced celery
4 c. diced potatoes
2 Tbsp. salt
1 Tbsp. Lawrys seasoning salt
1 Tbsp. onion chips or
   ¼ c. onions or ¼ tsp. onion salt
1 tsp. pepper
2-3 qt. milk
1½ Tbsp. chicken base
3-4 loaves toasted bread

Fry on chicken fryer and put in 20 qt. stock pots and keep warm in food warmers or oven.

Homemade Dressing (Stuffing)

271

MATTHEW & MARLENE TROYER

7 lg. loaves of bread toasted
   in butter
27 eggs
3 qt. turkey with broth
2 qt. vegetable mixture,
   potatoes & carrots
celery salt or cut-up celery
3 qt. milk
½ c. chicken base, approx.

Toast bread, 2 loaves per 1 stick of real butter. Beat eggs and add rest of ingredients. Add to toasted bread which has been put in a large bowl. Let set for at least ½ hour. Fry in a small amount of butter. This will fill an electric roaster. Serves 75.

Large Quantity

Noodles

VERNON & RUTH YODER

1½ gal. water
1½ gal. broth–4 (48 oz.) cans
½ can chicken base
1½ tsp. salt per lb. pkg. noodles
½ lb. butter
5 lb. med. noodles
1 lg. can cream of chicken soup
½-1 lb. Velveeta cheese

Bring water, broth, chicken base, salt and butter to a boil. Add noodles. Heat cream of chicken soup and cheese separately. When cheese is melted, add to noodles and let set for 1 hour. This makes 1 canner.

Chicken Noodles

MARY LENGACHER

5 qt. chicken broth
¼ c. seasoning salt
1 c. chicken base
3 cans cream of chicken soup
5 lb. Inn Maid noodles

Fill 5 gal. stock pot ¾ full with chicken broth and water. Boil. Add seasoning salt and chicken base. Add noodles. Bring to a boil, turn off heat, cover and let set 20 minutes. Add soup and serve. Serves 100.

272

Noodles (20 qt.)

MATTHIAS & NAOMI MAST

1 lb. butter, browned
5 (48 oz.) cans chicken broth
4 (48 oz.) cans water
5 sm. cans cream of chicken soup
¾ c. chicken base
2 Tbsp. salt
1 Tbsp. Lawry's
1 tsp. pepper
10 (8 oz.) pkg. Inn Maid noodles

In 20 qt. canner brown butter, add broth, water and remaining ingredients except noodles, and bring to a boil. Add noodles, bring to a boil, then turn off heat. Cover and let set for 2-3 hours. Serves 80 to 100.

Chicken & Noodles (20 qt.)

LUKE & KATHRYN MILLER

5 qt. chicken & broth,
   fill to ¾ full with water
1 c. chicken base
2 Tbsp. Lawry's salt
salt & pepper
5 lb. noodles
4 cans cream of chicken soup

Bring chicken, broth and seasonings to a boil; add noodles. Bring to a boil again. Cover and let set ½ hour. Add soups. Let set another ½hour-1 hour. Serves 100.

273

Mashed Potatoes

PAUL & NAOMI MAST

To 1-6 qt. kettle of potatoes add:
4 oz. cream cheese
4 Tbsp. butter
½ can evaporated milk
2 Tbsp. salt
3 c. hot milk

Herb Potatoes

IVAN & BARBARA SCHLABACH

potatoes, cubed
2 lb. butter
6 Tbsp. garlic salt
6 Tbsp. parsley
4 Tbsp. minced onion
1 Tbsp. salt
1 Tbsp. pepper

Fill electric roaster with potatoes. Mix seasoning together and sprinkle on potatoes, put butter on top. Bake at 400° till heated through. Stir often the first hour. When starting to soften turn down to 325° and don't stir often. Bake 4 hours. Serves 75.

Herb Potatoes

ENOS & NANCY TROYER

28 lb. potatoes
2 lb. butter
6 Tbsp. garlic salt
6 Tbsp. parsley flakes
4 Tbsp. minced onion
1 Tbsp. salt
1 Tbsp. pepper

If you have new potatoes, leave skins on. Wash and cut (or peel and cut) into 1" cubes. Add all the rest and you will have an electric roaster full. Bake at 250° about 2½ hours, stirring occasionally. Serves 50 to 60.

274

Potatoes

MATTHEW & MARLENE TROYER

20 lb. cooked, peeled &
    shredded potatoes
2 lb. butter
3 lb. cheese (like Velveeta)
4 cans cream of chicken soup
16 oz. sour cream

Put everything in electric roaster, except potatoes. Heat slowly until melted, then add cold potatoes. If you're making this a day ahead, be sure to cool it right away. Serves 75.

Potluck Potatoes

JOSEPH & RHODA MILLER

10 lb. potatoes
¾ c. butter
1 c. flour
2 qt. milk
3 Tbsp. salt
2 Tbsp. Lawry's salt
1 Tbsp. garlic salt
2 tsp. Liquid Smoke
2 (10.5 oz.) cans cream of chicken soup
2 c. sour cream
1 lb. Velveeta cheese
1½ lb. cubed ham

Cook potatoes till almost soft; shred. Make white sauce with butter, flour and milk; add seasonings, soup, sour cream and Velveeta cheese. Mix sauce with potatoes and ham. Bake at 350° for 1½ hours. Serves 30.

Chicken Spaghetti

ENOS & NANCY TROYER

4 lb. spaghetti
4 (10 oz.) cans cream of
  mushroom soup
4 (10 oz.) cans cream of chicken
  soup
1 sm. jar pimientos (optional)
1 c. butter
1 box Velveeta cheese
2 med. onions, chopped
4 c. chopped celery
2 c. chopped green & red sweet
  peppers
chili powder
salt
pepper
chicken

Cook spaghetti lightly; sauté peppers, celery and onions in butter. Mix all together and add chili powder, salt and pepper to taste. Cut Velveeta cheese in small chunks so as to melt better. If too thick add chicken broth instead of milk. Cook as much chicken as you like, with broth, then cut into small pieces. This will fill an electric roaster. Serves 75.

275

Large Quantity

Potluck Potatoes

MATTHIAS & NAOMI MAST

12 lb. potatoes, shredded &
  cooked in salt water
1 c. butter
½-¾ c. flour
1 pt. sour cream
3 sm. cans cream of chicken soup
1 tsp. pepper
2 tsp. salt
6 c. milk
1¼ lb. Velveeta cheese

Melt butter; add flour. Blend until smooth. Add sour cream, chicken soup, pepper, salt and milk; heat until thickened, then add Velveeta cheese. Mix with potatoes. May be topped with crushed crackers, toasted in melted butter. For a different variety, add 2 lb. fried hamburger with 2 Tbsp. taco seasoning.

Sloppy Joes

9 lb. hamburger
4 c. chopped onions
4 c. chopped celery
4 c. oatmeal
4½ c. milk
5½ c. ketchup
4 c. tomato juice
¾ c. brown sugar
¼ c. vinegar
5 Tbsp. Worcestershire sauce
3 Tbsp. mustard
3 Tbsp. salt
1 tsp. pepper

Brown hamburger and onions, then add the rest of the ingredients. Mix all together and bake at 300° for 1½ hours.

276

Meatball Mashed Potato Casserole

MATTHIAS & NAOMI MAST

20 lb. hamburger, made into
  your favorite meatballs
barbecue sauce

2-6 qt. & 1-8 qt.
  mashed potatoes
3 (8 oz.) pkg. cream cheese
1½ c. butter
salt to taste
garlic salt to taste

Sauce:
3 qt. milk
1½ c. flour
4 Tbsp. Worcestershire sauce
2 (26 oz.)cans cream of
  mushroom soup

2 tsp. seasoning salt
1 box Velveeta cheese
1 tsp. onion salt

In bottom of 2 electric roasters, divide meatballs, layer with barbecue sauce (I used homemade). Heat milk; thicken with flour. Add Worcestershire sauce, salts, cheese and soup, divide on top of meatballs. Cook and mash potatoes; add cream cheese, butter and salt. 1 cream cheese and 1 butter per kettle.

Underground Ham Casserole

277

MATTHIAS & NAOMI MAST

6 Tbsp. butter
1½ Tbsp. Worcestershire sauce
¾ c. chopped onion
8 c. chopped or cubed ham
3 cans cream of mushroom soup
3 c. Velveeta cheese
6 qt. potatoes, cooked & mashed
1 c. milk
1½ pt. sour cream
4 oz. cream cheese
bacon bits

Melt butter; add onion, ham and Worcestershire sauce; heat until onions are tender, add soup and cheese. When cheese is melted put in bottom of roaster. Mash potatoes; add milk, sour cream, salt and cream cheese. Spoon on top of gravy, starting around the edge so that gravy does not push to the top. Garnish with cheese and bacon bits. Bake at 200° till heated through. Recipe makes Lifetime roaster ¾ full.

Large Quantity

Haystacks

MATTHIAS & NAOMI MAST

20 lb. hamburger
3 c. brown sugar
6 Tbsp. taco seasoning
3 qt. baked beans
6 qt. pizza sauce
6 pt. sour cream
3 boxes crackers, crushed
7 bags nacho chips, crushed
8 pt. pepper rings
2 (8 qt.) cheese sauce
2 fix-n-mix bowls lettuce
10 c. rice, uncooked

Brown hamburger, mix with brown sugar, taco seasoning, baked beans and pizza sauce. Prepare cheese sauce (recipe follows), cut up lettuce, and cook rice. Serves 110.

Cheese Sauce

MATTHIAS & NAOMI MAST

278

1 c. butter
2¼ c. flour
2 tsp. Lawry's salt, heaping
2 tsp. taco seasoning
1 tsp. salt
1 gal. milk
1½-2 lb. Velveeta cheese
sour cream

In 6 qt. kettle melt butter, blend in flour until smooth; add milk slowly, stirring constantly. Heat until thickened, then add Lawry's salt, taco seasoning and salt. Add Velvetta cheese. You can add sour cream, salsa or taco sauce for added flavor.

Frogmore Stew

The Yucky Stuff (broth):
1 c. ketchup
1 c. vegetable oil
1 c. vinegar
1 (3 oz.) pkg. crab boil seasoning
(use the kind that comes in a
bag—available at Wal-Mart)
¾ c. salt
(broth should be very salty)
2 tsp. black pepper
16 c. water

The Good Stuff:
6 lb. chicken tenders, cut in bite
size pcs.
5 lb. sausage links, cut in bite
size pcs.
2 lb. precooked shrimp, thawed
12 potatoes, cut in wedges,
not sliced, don't peel
1-2 green peppers, sliced
(optional)
12 oz. pkg. mushrooms, whole
(optional)
3 lg. onions, cut in wedges
1½ lb. baby carrots or
sliced carrots

Dinner or suppertime: Lunch was at 12:00 - this is how we did it. Turn burner on high all the time. 10:30 put broth in canner when it boils.

Keep boiling all the time!

11:05 add potatoes

11:10 sausage

11:20 chicken

11:40 mushrooms & onions

11:50 shrimp & peppers

12:00 turn off burner, let set 5 minutes with lid on. Have people seated and ready to eat. Strain off broth and pour down middle of table which is lined with foil or cookie sheets. *Dip:* ketchup, sour cream, ranch dressing or your choice. *Tips:* Have stuff cut up and line up as you dump it in canner. Have people there 15 minutes or so before you expect to have stew ready. Stew is best if served as soon as it's ready. *Before adding shrimp etc. check to see if meat and taters are ready. If they aren't done wait another 5 minutes or so, before adding the last ingredients. Relax, it's easy. And make adjustments as needed. *Dinner rolls and ice cream go well with it. No spoons, forks, or plates needed, delicious and handy. We had 2 canners for our family of 29 people. Was plenty to each take home yet and was delicious warmed. Enjoy!

279

Sauce for Grilled Chicken

MATTHEW & MARLENE TROYER

20 lb. chicken, marinated
   in Italian dressing
1 pt. water
1 pt. vinegar
3 Tbsp. salt
1 Tbsp. Worcestershire sauce
1½-2 c. brown sugar

Bring to a boil everything except chicken. Thicken a little with clear jel mixed with a little water. Put on layers of chicken as it's grilled. Then bake or cook slowly till ready to eat.

Seasoning for 10 lb. Pork

MATTHIAS & NAOMI MAST

⅓ c. salt
2 tsp. sage
1¼ tsp. black pepper
¾ tsp. red pepper
¼ c. brown sugar
⅓ c. Liquid Smoke
1 tsp. curry powder
1¼ tsp. coriander
3 tsp. fennel seed (optional)

280

Chili Soup

MICHAEL & JOANNE COBLENTZ

6 lb. hamburger
2 lb. sausage
4 qt. water
8 qt. tomato juice
4 c. ketchup
2 cans beans
4 c. brown sugar
4 c. flour
4 Tbsp. salt
3 Tbsp. seasoned salt
2½ Tbsp. chili powder

Brown hamburger and sausage with some onions. In 20 qt. canner heat juice and water. Bring to a boil. Add hamburger, sausage, ketchup and beans. Mix sugar and flour together and add enough water to make a paste. Slowly add to soup, mixing well. Add seasonings. Simmer for 30 minutes. This fills a canner.

Corn

1 c. butter
7 qt. corn
7 tsp. salt

Put butter in bottom of Lifetime roaster. Put in oven and melt butter, then add corn. Bake at 300° for 3 hours.

281

Vegetable Tray

MATTHIAS & NAOMI MAST

For 1 lg. vegetable tray:
1 head broccoli
1 head cauliflower
1 stalk celery
2 bags baby carrots
3 lg. peppers
3 cucumbers
1 cont. mushrooms
2 boxes grape tomatoes

Large Quantity

Taco Salad

7 heads lettuce
7 lb. hamburger, fried with
   11¼ Tbsp. taco seasoning
4 pkg. taco chips
3½ lb. shredded cheddar cheese
tomatoes (optional)

Dressing:
1 qt. Miracle Whip
7 Tbsp. taco seasoning
1 c. sugar
1 bottle Thousand Island dressing
7 Tbsp. taco sauce

Mix only minutes before serving, adding chips the very last. Yield: 4 (13 qt.) mixing bowls.

Dill Pickles for Church

MATTHIAS & NAOMI MAST

If you don't have enough canned pickles for church, buy 1 gal. dill pickles and add 8 Tbsp. vinegar and 4 c. sugar. Mix together in large bowl. Let set for a few days.

282

Fruit & Glaze

MARY LENGACHER

6 gal. peaches, sliced, cut in
    thirds
4 gal. fruit cocktail
2 gal. pineapple tidbits
2 gal. mandarin oranges
4 lb. red grapes, sliced in half
4 lb. green grapes, sliced in half

Drain juice from all fruit and save. Do not use mandarin orange juice for this recipe. Heat juices and thicken with Perma-Flo. Add rest of ingredients and pour over fruit. Refrigerate. Serves 400.

Glaze:
fruit juices
4 c. Perma-Flo
¼ c. ReaLemon
2 tsp. vanilla

4-6 c. sugar
¼ tsp. salt
3 c. vanilla instant pudding

Pie Crust (Flaky)

ENOS & NANCY TROYER

283

8 c. Flaky pastry flour
3 c. Crisco
4 tsp. salt
1 c. cold water

Mix flour, Crisco and salt by hand till crumbly. Add cold water. This makes 12 crusts (or 6 double crust pies).

Strawberry Pie Filling

PAUL & NAOMI MAST

1 lg. box strawberry Jell-O
1 box strawberry Danish Dessert
1¾ c. sugar
4 Tbsp. clear jel, rounded

Mix clear jel with 1 c. cold water and pour into 4 c. hot water; add 1 tsp. ReaLemon and 4 Tbsp. Karo. 1 recipe makes 3 pies.

Large Quantity

Pecan Pie

ENOS & NANCY TROYER

9 doz. eggs
36 c. Karo
18 c. sugar
12 Tbsp. vanilla
5½ c. butter, melted
pecans

Beat all together, except pecans. Use approx. ¾ c. pecans per pie. Yield: 36 pies. Serves 325.

Butterscotch Sauce

ENOS & NANCY TROYER

10 c. hot water
7 c. brown sugar
dash of salt
2 c. water, mixed with
   1¼ c. clear jel (cook type)

When first 3 ingredients come to a boil, add clear jel mixture. Cook and stir till thickened. Add 3 Tbsp. vanilla and 1 c. butter. This is good to use with date pudding, etc. Yield: 1 gal.

284

Large Cake Mix

STEVE & MIRIAM LENGACHER

1 cake mix
1 egg
⅓ c. flour
1 tsp. baking powder
¾ c. water
½ c. sugar
1 Tbsp. cooking oil

Mix and bake according to directions on box.

Menus

Breakfast Menus

FOOD ITEM:	AMOUNT:
butterhorns	10-11 doz.
breakfast casserole	3½-4 Lifetime roasters
fresh & thickened fruit	4 lg. bowls (fix-n-mix)
baked goods (breakfast style)	6 (11"x17") pans
orange juice	7½-8 gal.

Served for Sunday lunch. Adults and children mixed. Used 1 Lifetime roaster potatoes, cooked, shredded and fried, 12 dozen scrambled eggs, 8 qt. sausage gravy and cheese sauce for casserole. Amount served to 150 people.

JACOB & LORETTA WEAVER

FOOD ITEM:	AMOUNT:
breakfast casserole	1 electric + 1 Lifetime roaster
french toast	70 pieces
baked goods	5 (10"x15") sheet cakes
mixed fruit	2 fix-n-mix bowls

Amount served to 75 people.

IVAN & BARBARA SCHLABACH

286

Lunch and Dinner Menus

FOOD ITEM:	AMOUNT:
herb potatoes	1 electric roaster
barbecued meatballs	10 lb.
corn	7 qt.
applesauce	3½ qt.
strawberries & peaches	2½ qt.
sheet cakes	4
ice cream	2 pails

Served at hot lunch, birthday party. Around 45 children. Amount served to 75 people.

IVAN & BARBARA SCHLABACH

FOOD ITEM:	AMOUNT:
mashed potatoes	10 qt.
chicken gravy	4 qt.
barbecued meatballs (small)	10 lb. hamburger
corn	4 qt.
7-layer salad	Tupperware cake taker
cake with fruit	2 (11"x17") pans
(cream cheese filling)	
ice cream	2 pails

Served on a warm 88° day for a men and boys' work day. Served iced coffee and homemade root beer in the afternoon. Amount served to 40 people.

MATTHIAS & NAOMI MAST

FOOD ITEM:	AMOUNT:
meatball mashed potato casserole	
salad	
fruit	
turtle cake	
whipped ice cream	

MATTHIAS & NAOMI MAST

FOOD ITEM:	AMOUNT:
potluck potatoes with ham	2 electric roasters ¾ full
barbecued green beans	1 (2 gal.) roaster
Chinese cabbage	4 heads cabbage
pumpkin torte	6 (9"x13") pans
ice cream	3 pails

Amount served to 95 people.

MATTHIAS & NAOMI MAST

FOOD ITEM:	AMOUNT:
yummasetti	2 electric roasters & 1 (6 qt.) kettle
peas	19 lb.
salads	9 fix-n-mix bowls
fruit delights	10 lg. cake takers

Served at bishop ordination Nov. 12, 2011. Amount served to 183 people.

FOOD ITEM:	AMOUNT:
yumezetti	2 electric roasters
green beans	20 qt.
mixed fruit	4½ fix-n-mix bowls
cookies	20 doz.
applesauce	6 qt.
banana peppers	¾ gal.

This was for Sunday noon. Our community has lots of children. Amount served to 150 people.

JAY & AMY TROYER

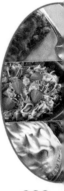

FOOD ITEM:	AMOUNT:
yumasetti	4 gal. or 2 Lifetime roasters
barbecued green beans	2 gal. or 1 Lifetime roaster
applesauce	8 qt.
cake delights	5 (11"x17") pans
(cream cheese & fruit filling)	
Served at a viewing.	

MATTHIAS & NAOMI MAST

FOOD ITEM:	AMOUNT:
chickenetti	2 (17 qt.) electric roasters
green beans with barbecue sauce	20 qt. beans/3 qt. barbecue sauce
lettuce salad	5 fix-n-mix bowls
brownies	6 (11"x17") pans
hot fudge sauce	4 qt.
ice cream	3½ gal.

Served for a Sunday School lunch crowd. Amount served to 140 people.

VERNON & RUTH YODER

Menus

FOOD ITEM:	AMOUNT:
chicken spaghetti	1 heaping electric roaster (18 qt.)
barbecued green beans	13-14 qt.
salads	4 fix-n-mix bowls
variety of desserts	6 lg. cake taker size

Served for Sunday evening supper. Amount served to 148 people.

JACOB & LORETTA WEAVER

FOOD ITEM:	AMOUNT:
spaghetti pie	17 qt. electric roaster/6 qt. casserole dish
corn	9 qt.
lettuce salad	4 fix-n-mix bowls
fruit pizza	6 (11"x17") pans

Served for a supper and singing crowd. Amount served to 100 people.

VERNON & RUTH YODER

290

FOOD ITEM:	AMOUNT:
burrito casserole	2 electric roasters ¾ full
corn & peas	11 qt. & 1 bag peas
peaches/blueberries	12 qt. peaches, 2 qt. blueberries
strawberries	4 qt.
ice cream desserts	5 Tupperware cake takers

Amount served to 115 people.

MATTHIAS & NAOMI MAST

FOOD ITEM:	AMOUNT:
burrito casserole	18 qt. roaster ¾ full
corn	5 qt.
pasta salad	Thatsa bowl
frozen cheesecakes	2 (9"x13") pans
pumpkin pies	3
pecan pies	2

Sunday evening supper. Plenty left over. Amount served to 30 people.

SAMUEL & LEANNA WEAVER

FOOD ITEM:	AMOUNT:
burrito casserole	electric roaster + 1 small one
lettuce	2 fix-n-mix bowls
salsa	4 qt.
corn	7 qt.
ice cream dessert	4 cake takers

Amount served to 100 people.

JOSIAH & SUSAN MILLER

FOOD ITEM:	AMOUNT:
hobo's delight	4 gal.
shredded lettuce	2 fix-n-mix bowls
shredded cheese	4 lb.
corn chips	6 bags
Ranch dressing	4 bottles
noodles	used 4 (16 oz.) bags
Swiss Roll cakes	4 sheet pans
ice cream	3 pails

Amount served to 90 people.

MICHAEL & JOANNE COBLENTZ

291

Menus

FOOD ITEM:	AMOUNT:
22 lb. turkey	1 electric roaster
gourmet potatoes	1 electric roaster
frozen corn	6 qt. crockpot
vegetable pizza	3 (13"x18") pans
pumpkin crunch	4 (9"x13") pans
vanilla ice cream	3 gal.

We dressed and put the turkey in Tender Quick and liquid smoke and soaked it for 3 days. Roasted and deboned it and made enough gravy to fill roaster. Amount served to 58 people.

MATTHEW & MARLENE TROYER

292

Lite and Easy Menus

FOOD ITEM:	AMOUNT:
noodles	2 (20 qt.) stockpots
yogurt	4 (1 gal.) containers
apple sauce	1 gal.
fruit (fresh)	2 fix-n-mix bowls
cookies	20 doz.

Served for Communion lunch. A little more than 1 stockpot noodles would have been enough. 7 lb. Inn Maid noodles for 1 stockpot. Amount served to 150 people.

FOOD ITEM:	AMOUNT:
noodles	20 qt.
Big Mac sandwiches	100
vegetables & dip	2 heads cauliflower
	3 heads broccoli
	3 bags baby carrots
	3 bags radishes
	3 stalks celery
	2 cont. mushrooms
	9 cucumbers
	12 peppers
	2 cont. grape tomatoes
	8 lb. ranch dip
fruit pizza	4 (11"x17") pans

Amount served to 110 people.

MATTHIAS & NAOMI MAST

293

FOOD ITEM:	AMOUNT:
meat & cheese sandwiches	150
vegetables & dip	2 heads cauliflower
	2 heads broccoli
	3 bags baby carrots
	2 stalks celery
	8 peppers
	8 cucumbers
	2 cont. grape tomatoes
	6 pt. ranch dip
fruit smoothies	130 (6 oz.) cups
salt snacks	12 bags
cookies	13 doz.
coffee	
tea	

Served for a school field trip. For 130 (6 oz.) cups of fruit smoothies. I used 2 gal. yogurt, 4 qt. peaches, 20 bananas, 5 qt. strawberries, 1½ (46 oz.) cans pineapple juice, 2 qt. frozen blueberries. Amount served to 125 people.

MATTHIAS & NAOMI MAST

FOOD ITEM:	AMOUNT:
sloppy joe sandwiches	18 lb. hamburger
chicken & noodles	20 qt. stockpot
potato salad	3½ gal.
fruit or pudding delight	5 (9"x13") pans

A simple, but satisfying meal for a large crowd. Amount served to 100 people.

LUKE & KATHRYN MILLER

FOOD ITEM:	AMOUNT:
grilled hamburger sandwiches	12 lb. hamburger
chips	6 packs
pasta salad	½ fix-n-mix bowl
brownies	2 pans
ice cream	2 pails
toppings	

For hamburger sandwiches we had cheese, lettuce, onions, Miracle Whip, ketchup, mustard, relish and hot peppers. It doesn't take much of each. For toppings: we had M&M's, Heath bits, cashews, Oreo cookies, warm chocolate, warm caramel and warm butterscotch. Just a small container of each. This was for supper and singing. Amount served to 50 people.

JAY & AMY TROYER

FOOD ITEM:	AMOUNT:
chili soup	17 qt. electric roaster (full) or 20 qt. canner - not quite full
cheeseburger soup	17 qt. electric roaster (full) or 20 qt. canner - not quite full
bread sticks	17 doz.
corn chip salad	4-5 fix-n-mix bowls
fruit delights	6 lg. cake taker size pans

295

This was served for Sunday lunch. Amount served to 125 people.

MICHAEL & JOANNE COBLENTZ

FOOD ITEM:	AMOUNT:
cheeseburger soup	13-14 qt.
vegetables & dip	1 lg. tray
sliced meat & cheese	1 lg. platter
cakes	3
ice cream	2 pails

My notes concerning the amount needed said "about right." Amount served to 60 people.

JACOB & LORETTA WEAVER

Menus

FOOD ITEM:	AMOUNT:
country ham & potato soup	1½ electric roasters
chili soup	1 electric roaster & 4 qt.
bread sticks	300-2"x5"
vegetable pizza	7 (13"x18") pans
apple crisp	9 (9"x13") pans
ice cream	exactly 4 pails

This menu was used for Sunday noon. Some of the "apple" crisps were blueberry, peach or raspberry crisps. It took 6 boxes crackers. Amount served to 150 people.

JAY & AMY TROYER

296

FOOD ITEM:	AMOUNT:
country potato soup with ham	4½ gal.
crackers	3 boxes wheat roasted vegetable
salad bar	2 fix-n-mix bowls lettuce, cut up
	2 heads broccoli, chopped
	1 head cauliflower, chopped
	4 peppers, chopped
	5 cucumbers, cut up
	alfalfa & radish sprouts
	6 lb. bacon, fried & crumbled
	4 pk. Ramen noodles, crushed & toasted
	2 doz. hard-boiled eggs, cut up
	1 med. bowl shredded cheese
	4 c. onions
	2 c. sunflower seeds
	4 c. tomatoes
	1 bag spinach, cut up
	3 qt. homemade lettuce dressing
	simple salad dressing
	favorite salad dressing
	French dressing
frozen cheesecake with fruit topping	3 lg. Tupperware cake takers

Amount served to 70 people.

MATTHIAS & NAOMI MAST

Wedding Menus

FOOD ITEM:	AMOUNT:
dinner rolls	37 doz.
sweet & sour chicken	250 lb.
herb potatoes	6 electric roasters
peas & carrots	60 lb.
pasta salad	13 gal.
mini mocha cheesecakes	17 doz.
mini cheesecakes	25 doz.
fruit plates with dip	13 batches dip
ice cream cups	600

We canned our leftover chicken sauce. Made 1 gal. each lemon and grape pie filling for cheesecakes. Served at our daughter's wedding. Amount served to 400 people.

IVAN & BARBARA SCHLABACH

FOOD ITEM:	AMOUNT:
mashed potatoes	20 (6 qt.) kettles
dressing	9 (13 qt.) mixing bowls
gravy	7 gal.
corn	40 qt.
taco salad	4 (13 qt.) mixing bowls
apricot nectar salad	26 bowls
strawberry pie	

Used for a wedding of approximately 550 people. All recipes are found in the large quantity section.

Other Favorite Menus

RECIPE FOR _____
_____
_____
_____
_____
_____
_____
_____
_____
_____
_____
_____
_____
_____

RECIPE FOR _____
_____
_____
_____
_____
_____
_____
_____
_____
_____
_____
_____
_____
_____

Index

Beverages & Appetizers

Breads & Rolls

300

Breakfast

Soups & Vegetables

301

Salad & Salad Dressings

Index

Meats & Main Dishes

302

Pizza & Sandwiches

303

Index

Pies

Desserts

304

305

Canning & Freezing

Farmhouse Kitchen

307

Index

308

Farmhouse Kitchen

My Other Favorites

RECIPE FOR _____

_____
_____
_____
_____
_____
_____
_____
_____
_____
_____
_____

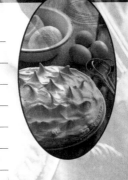

RECIPE FOR _____

_____
_____
_____
_____
_____
_____
_____
_____
_____
_____
_____
_____

My Other Favorites

RECIPE FOR

RECIPE FOR

My Other Favorites

RECIPE FOR _____

_____
_____
_____
_____
_____
_____
_____
_____
_____
_____
_____
_____

RECIPE FOR _____

_____
_____
_____
_____
_____
_____
_____
_____
_____
_____
_____

My Other Favorites

RECIPE FOR _____
_____
_____
_____
_____
_____
_____
_____
_____
_____
_____
_____
_____

RECIPE FOR _____
_____
_____
_____
_____
_____
_____
_____
_____
_____
_____
_____
_____

My Other Favorites

RECIPE FOR _____

_____
_____
_____
_____
_____
_____
_____
_____
_____

RECIPE FOR _____

_____
_____
_____
_____
_____
_____
_____
_____
_____
_____
_____

RECIPE FOR

RECIPE FOR